MICHEL TREMBLAY

THE GUID SISTERS
and other plays

THE GUID SISTERS
Translated by
Bill Findlay and Martin Bowman

MANON/SANDRA
Translated by John Van Burek

ALBERTINE IN FIVE TIMES
Translated by
John Van Burek and Bill Glassco

With an Introduction by Annika Bluhm

NICK HERN BOOKS
London

A Nick Hern Book

The Guid Sisters first published in Great Britain in 1991 as an original paperback by Nick Hern Books, a Random Century Company, 20 Vauxhall Bridge Road, London SW1V 2SA

Cover illustration derived from Pashke's *Hilda*, 1973. Reproduced by courtesy of Galerie Darthea Speyer, Paris

Printed in Great Britain by
T.J. Press (Padstow) Ltd, Padstow, Cornwall

British Library Cataloguing in Publication Data
A catalogue record for this book is available from the British Library

ISBN 1-85459-118-5

MICHEL TREMBLAY

Michel Tremblay was born in 1942 in Montreal's French-speaking industrial east end. Whilst at the Graphic Arts Institute of Quebec, where he trained as a linotypist, he began writing short stories, which were later published under the title *Stories for Late Night Drinkers*. In 1964 he won the first prize for young writers sponsored by the Canadian Broadcasting Corporation for his play, *Le Train*, written in 1959.

He first achieved national prominence in 1968 with the premiere of *Les Belles Soeurs*, written in *joual*, the popular patois of Quebec. Subsequently dubbed 'the single most important event in the history of Quebec theatre', the play has also been seen in Paris in 1973, where it was declared best foreign production of the year, and in a Scots version, *The Guid Sisters*, at the Tron Theatre, Glasgow, in 1989 and again in 1990. There followed a cycle of plays all set in Montreal mostly among homosexuals, transvestites and social misfits, often with characters reappearing from play to play. These include *Broken Pieces* (1969); *Forever Yours Marie-Lou* (1971); *Hosanna* (1973); *Sainte-Carmen of the Main* (1976); and *Manon/Sandra* (1977), which was seen at the Traverse, Edinburgh, in 1984, and in London in 1989. His move to Outremont, a more affluent district of Montreal, and the election of an independent Quebec government in 1976 seem to have influenced a shift in his writing, as demonstrated in plays such as *The Impromptu of Outremont* (1980), *Albertine in Five Times* (1984; seen in London in 1986) and *The Real World?* (1987; seen in London in 1990).

As well as plays – eighteen to date, most of which have also been translated and performed in English – Tremblay has written two musical comedies, eight novels and seven film scripts. His *Chroniques du Plateau Mont-Royal* is a sequence of novels about a working-class street in Montreal. *Making Room* was the first of his novels to be published in Britain (1990). Tremblay has also translated and adapted plays by Aristophanes, Tennessee Williams, Dario Fo, Chekhov and Gogol. A complete chronology of his work appears inside this volume.

Contents

Introduction

This volume broadly covers the best of Michel Tremblay's playwriting to date. Each of the three plays can be seen as indicative of a stage in his development as a dramatist. *Les Belles-Soeurs*, written in 1965, was his first full-length play and immediately placed Tremblay in the vanguard of new Québecois writing when it was given its premiere in Montreal in 1968. It is printed here in its Scots version, *The Guid Sisters*, first seen in Glasgow in 1989. *Manon/Sandra (Damnée Manon Sacrée Sandra)*, written and first performed in 1977, marks the end of a cycle of plays which began with *Les Belles-Soeurs*. It had its British premiere at the Man in the Moon pub theatre in London in 1989. And the final play in the collection, *Albertine in Five Times (Albertine en cinq temps)*, comes from the second phase of Tremblay's writing, which began in 1981. Written in 1984, it played to wide acclaim and won the Chalmers Canadian Plays Award for 1985. It was first seen in Britain in 1986 in a production by the Tarragon Theatre from Toronto, who performed both in Edinburgh and at the Donmar Theatre, London.

To appreciate Tremblay's work it is important to have an understanding of the theatrical and cultural milieu from which he came. Although there had been some noteworthy work in the 'forties and 'fifties by French-Canadian writers – notably Gratien Gélinas, who had written in the Québecois dialect and placed it on stage as early as 1938 with 'Fridolinons', a series of revue sketches which eventually developed into his full-length play, *Tit-Coq* – it wasn't until the Quiet Revolution, begun in 1959, that Quebec theatre really came of age. The Quiet Revolution, marked by the death of Maurice Duplessis (leader of the Union Nationale) and the election of Jean Lesage's Liberals in 1960, was a time of great cultural growth during which Quebec began to develop a sense of its own identity and culture, separate from that of English-Canada. In terms of theatre, although several new companies had been formed in the 'fifties, the work was mainly limited to productions of the classics with little indigenous work. As the Quiet Revolution became noisier the demand grew for more nationalistic writing both on the stage and in novels. This was a time of 'cultural liberation' for the people of Quebec – both

Gratien Gélinas and Marcel Dubé had moved away from the working class and had begun writing for the Quebec middle class, while younger writers such as Françoise Loranger and Robert Gurik began to write for a nationalist and feminist audience, rejecting the middle class refinement of established theatre in favour of a more left-wing, working class realism. This was exemplified by their controversial use of *joual*.

As early as 1964 certain publishing houses were beginning to produce work written in phonetic *joual*. *Joual* (the word is a corruption of the French for horse, *cheval*, and is a slang-derived form of Québecois that uses many anglicised words) was touted as the language of the people – the truly indigenous language which gave Quebecers a sense of identity. Tremblay's decision in 1965 to write *Les Belles-Soeurs* in *joual* was an explosive move, dividing critics between those who applauded both its language and its depiction of the working class tenements of Montreal and those who were scandalized by the vulgarity of *joual* and Tremblay's characters. It was an instant and controversial hit, catapulting the young Tremblay to celebrity status along with his director, André Brassard. They became a symbol for the nationalists who believed, amongst other things, that one of the ways to help Quebec find its identity was to stop talking in a language that had been imposed on them.

The seventies was a time of great expansion in indigenous writing – aided by the proliferation of alternative theatres, frequently nationalistic, which aimed to return theatre to the people, to 'democratise the theatrical experience'. Writers such as Jean Barbeau and Michel Garneau began to write in *joual* about working class subjects, although it was Tremblay who dominated the theatrical scene throughout the seventies as he continued to explore the lives of repressed minorities, specifically working class women living on the rue Fabre, where Tremblay himself grew up, and transvestites congregating in the bars of The Main, Montreal's red light district. All these characters face deprivation emotionally, financially and spiritually. They can also be seen as metaphors for Quebec. In *Forever Yours Marie Lou (A toi pour toujours, ta Marie-Lou)* the parents represent Quebec's hopeless, paralysed past, their two daughters respectively the ineffectual present and the hope of a liberating future. In *Hosanna*, the night of crisis that Hosanna goes through as she searches for and eventually comes to terms with her own identity is reflected in the Quebec people's own identity crisis. Tremblay is quoted as saying: 'We submitted to a foreign culture and this turned us into transvestites . . . Quebec culture had all sorts of disguises to keep its heart and roots from being seen.'

Tremblay's *Belles-Soeurs* cycle of plays which ended in 1977 with *Manon/Sandra*, coincided roughly with the election of the Parti Québecois in late 1976. Although this cycle of plays can be linked to the political climate of the time they are not and never were merely political diatribes advocating separatism. Speaking of the early plays he has said, 'If they were political, it was because of the social background. I don't like political theatre, I like political fables.'

Tremblay was born in 1942 into a working class family in the Plateau Mont-Royal section of Montreal. His father was a printing press operator and Michel studied graphic arts after high school before becoming a linotype operator, a trade which he pursued from 1963–1966 – a trade now overtaken by computer typesetting. His first play was *Le Train*, written in 1960, a one-act which won the 1964 CBC competition for young authors. It interested André Brassard, a young actor/director who established a fertile working relationship with Tremblay which survives to this day. The two young men were united in their antipathy to the 'international' French spoken in mainstream theatre and in their desire to give a voice to the Montreal working class. Tremblay has always written about the people of Montreal, specifically the working classes, feeling that his universality as a writer comes through his locality. 'I want to go on writing for exactly the same people for whom I wrote *Les Belles-Soeurs* in '65. I think that's very important and it's the only way in which my national audience also can grow . . . I don't write for the whole world, I've never wanted to write for the whole world, I write for the people who live right here.'

Tremblay wrote *Les Belles-Soeurs* in 1965 but it was another three years before André Brassard could persuade anyone to take the risk of staging it. In early 1968 Tremblay was in Mexico on a Canada Council grant writing his first novel, but he rushed home when Brassard managed to get the play staged in August 1968 at the Théâtre du Rideau Vert in Montreal. From this time Tremblay's output was prolific; not only original work for the stage and for television but also adaptations and translations of plays by other authors. He also began writing novels.

Himself a practising homosexual in a predominantly heterosexual society, Tremblay reflects in his plays an understanding of and sensitivity towards other repressed minorities, specifically women. All of his plays explore human beings forced by sexual preference, sexual repression, class or poverty to live on the margins of society. They are stories of incestuous love, transvestism, sexual repression and madness as well as of the struggle to find love, a sense of spirituality and pride in one's own identity. The unspoken, unforced parallel with the separatist ideals of Quebec is clear, though the plays themselves are intensely focused on their characters' private lives and emotions.

After the *Belles-Soeurs* cycle, Tremblay took a break from playwriting for three years. In 1981 he returned with *The Impromptu of Outremont* (*L'Impromptu d'Outremont*) – a strong attack on the middle class bourgeoisie who pined for the culture that had been smashed by such writers as Tremblay and yet were paralysed by society and incapable of fighting back. It is the least sympathetic and compassionate of his plays. His later plays have less of the anger and force of his work in the seventies, possibly partly due to the more relaxed political climate, possibly because Tremblay himself simply wished to move on. Throughout his work he has returned to explore his own childhood – most notably in *Albertine* and through a series of semi-autobiographical novels, known as *Les Chroniques du Plateau Mont-Royal*, after his birthplace.

The majority of his plays and novels use a device which has become a hallmark of Tremblay's writing: namely the further development of characters already introduced and explored in earlier works. Manon in *Manon/Sandra* is the tormented daughter of Marie Lou, Sandra was Hosanna's cruel joker, La Duchesse, from an early monologue, appears again in *Hosanna* and is murdered in *Sainte-Carmen of the Main* (*Sainte Carmen de la Main*). This technique has been picked up by English-Canadian writers, notably David French with his Mercer plays and James Reaney with The Donnellys. Tremblay believes that since he himself 'always remains the same person, why not keep the same characters and try to go further with them. Since you yourself have gone further with what you want to say, why not make them do the same?'.

As well as re-using his characters Tremblay has remained faithful to his native city, Montreal, the setting for all his plays: 'I am giving myself the task, from now up to the end of my days, to prove that it is possible to write about anything, everything, by simply writing about ourselves, within one city.' Local as the plays are in situation, the themes they embrace are universal – love, family loyalty and the struggle for life in the face of emotional and financial difficulty. And as a result, their appeal goes beyond French-Canada, as witness successful productions in France, England and Scotland.

Stylistically Tremblay is also by no means narrow. He will combine Québecois (the most naturalistic of dialects) with highly stylized Greek-like choral work and Brechtian moments of alienation as the characters talk directly to the audience. And he will play with voices in different time periods within the same scene. This last is a theatrical device that he employs many times but always differently. For example the five Albertines, all at different stages of their lives, converse freely with each other on stage, whilst Serge in *Bonjour, là, Bonjour*, moves between different locations and times within the same scene while continuously talking to his family.

Tremblay is a theatrical writer in an auditory rather than a visual sense. Throughout his writing there are musical parallels, inspired by opera, string quartets and symphonies. Time and again his plays resemble musical composition. 'I have the plan at the beginning even if it isn't down on paper . . . I know what I have to say and as soon as I sit down to write, I can let myself go completely. I know that the structure of the play is going to be all right, I don't need to think about it anymore. So when I sit down to write, it really is music, I'm writing music, that's all – the structure of the play comes by itself.' *Bonjour, là, Bonjour* is written as a series of scenes each headed with a title, such as Trio, Octet, Quartet and so on, indicating the number of people speaking in the 'movement'. *Manon/Sandra* is written as a duet in which the two different themes of religion and sex are explored until their differences submerge and their similarities emerge to become an anthem for the two separate individuals. And from the very start of *Forever Yours Marie Lou*, as Renate Usmiani points out in the 1977 *Canadian Theatre Review*, the melody of each character is musically established, intertwined and developed as in a quartet.

MARIE LOU. Tomorrow . . .
CARMEN. Wow . . .
LÉOPOLD. Yeah . . .
MANON. Still . . .
    Silence.
MARIE LOU. Tomorrow we gotta . . .
CARMEN. Wow, it's already . . .
LÉOPOLD. Yeah, I know . . .
MANON. Still, it feels . . .
    Silence.

MARIE LOU. Tomorrow we gotta go eat at mother's . . .
CARMEN. Wow, it's already ten years . . .
LÉOPOLD. Yeah, I know . . . What a pain in the ass.
MANON. Still, it feels like yesterday . . .

The first of the three plays in this collection is *The Guid Sisters* (*Les Belles-Soeurs*), a comedy set in a Montreal tenement building. Germaine Lauzon has won a million stamps, which she must paste into books and which can then be exchanged for goods. She invites her female relations and friends to a pasting party at which they all begin to express their jealousy and bemoan the difficulty of their lives. One by one they begin to pilfer the booklets until Germaine notices that the books are missing and confronts the other women, attempting to force them to return the stamps. An enormous fight breaks out in which Germaine tries to prevent the women from leaving with her prize. Germaine is left standing alone, all the stamps gone, and, in a surrealistic ending, stamps rain down on her as she joins with the other women in singing 'O Canada'. This play already contains many of Tremblay's favourite devices. For instance, he borrows a chorus from the classics but has the chorus leader speaking naturalistically, most notably in the 'stupid, rotten life' refrain of the first act and the Ode to Bingo in the second act. The choral element serves to bind the women together giving their language a musicality and poetry. In moments of alienation the characters step out of the action to talk directly to the audience, revealing their innermost feelings. The surreal ending is indicative of Tremblay's love of theatricality: 'One can put right in the middle of a realistic scene an image which is totally absurd or totally transposed. And the public is going to accept it because the theatre is made for just that – to transform. My plays often end on a very strong image.' Also typical is that the play can be seen on several different levels; on one level it is simply a comedy about a group of women, on another it's a moral fable, on another it is a metaphor for Quebec, and on yet another it is a satire on the religion of consumerism. André Brassard is quoted as saying: 'Michel is an artistic director's dream. The educated public can find layers of meaning, but he also offers an entertaining evening of theatre for people who want just that.'

Tremblay is not proprietorial about his work and is very open to its being adapted and made accessible to different audiences. To this end he gives very few stage directions in his writing, leaving staging decisions up to the actors and the director. Similarly he is said to approve of the Scots version of *Les Belles-*

Soeurs. Scots has a muscularity and an energy similar to that of *joual*, and it gives the play a vigour and force which is not so apparent in a standard English translation. There are many similarities between Scotland and Quebec: their populations are almost the same; they are both bordered by a larger, English-speaking state which dominates politically, economically and culturally; both have a history of antagonism towards the dominant state, sometimes leading to warfare; there is a strong separatist movement in both countries against their larger neighbours; and both the Scots and the Quebecers have their own muscular, vigorous language which is seen as vulgar and unacceptable by the intelligentsia.

In *Manon/Sandra* Tremblay unites the worlds of the rue Fabre and The Main in the two characters of Manon and Sandra. Manon, from *Forever Yours Marie Lou*, lives in her mother's room on the rue Fabre and is obsessed with religion. Sandra has returned to the rue Fabre from The Main and is obsessed by sex. As both pursue their search for ecstasy through their obsessions, their monologues interweave, exploring the similarities and differences between them. Although seeming to be polar opposites at times they merge and become one another. Sandra talks of sex in religious terms:

SANDRA. To submit oneself to the Black, to yield to Him, sacrifice to Him, the purest, the most sacred image of our degenerate civilization.

whilst Manon speaks to God as to a lover:

MANON. I have a right to my pleasures! I'm used to them now! I like what You did for me and I want it to continue! You don't just ask a poor girl to sacrifice herself for fifteen years and then drop her!

Towards the end of the play Sandra reveals that 'she' was Manon's childhood friend of twenty years ago but cannot reveal herself to Manon after her years of debauchery as a transvestite. At the end of the play both characters realise that they have been 'invented by Michel' and are reconciled within him. Tremblay is quoted as seeing *Manon/Sandra* as part of a cycle of plays which took shape while writing *Forever Yours Marie Lou* when he realised that 'I'd have to do something about Carmen and Manon (the two girls in *Marie Lou*, a country singer and a religious fanatic) because as much as Carmen was right, in that play, representing a sort of solution, she wasn't right at all from another point of view'. In *Manon/Sandra* Tremblay marries the most poetic with the most crude of language. Manon's religious fervour is contrasted with Sandra's almost pornographic fantasies, but both characters talk with energy and passion – their obsessions are their life blood giving them vigour and the will to continue. Again, the subject matter is bleak but avoids pathos through the vitality and compassion of his writing.

In *Albertine in Five Times*, five actresses portray Albertine at different times of her life whilst all conversing freely together simultaneously. Albertine at thirty is recuperating in the country after viciously beating her eleven-year-old daughter; Albertine at forty is a virago, trapped in her house on the rue Fabre and in battle with the world; Albertine at fifty has rejected her past by re-inventing it and appears calm and happy; Albertine at sixty has found this false happiness impossible to sustain and has given in to depression, sitting in her room and taking tranquillizers; Albertine at seventy has found a kind of peace by coming to terms with the difficulty and fury of her life. The older Albertines advise the younger ones on what will happen, while the younger Albertines are full of life and passion. Between their conversations with each other and with their sister Madeleine, who acts as confidante to all of them, the Albertines portray an 'ordinary' woman's life, showing her struggle to live. Once more there are similarities between this later play and his earlier work – there is the same bleak life on the rue Fabre, there is a woman repressed by circumstance who nevertheless reacts with passion and energy. Tremblay portrays Albertine without sentimentality and without being patronising, and her life, although far from perfect, is given dignity by his compassion. There is little 'action' as such, but a sense of dramatic tension and climax is achieved through the juxtaposition of the quintet of different voices from different times, each with their own particular melody. *Albertine* belongs to a period of writing when Tremblay had begun to explore his own family in greater depth, and this play is based on the life of his Aunt Robertine. Tremblay has felt some guilt about using his family in this way and has sought to expiate this guilt in his 1988 play, *The Real World?* (*Le Vrai Monde?*), in which a young writer has to take responsibility for the effect that his writing has on his family.

Tremblay is one of the most acclaimed playwrights that Quebec in particular and Canada in general has produced in the last twenty years. His plays have been translated into seven languages and produced on four continents, and he inspires an almost reverential admiration from much of the theatre community and the public. In 1977 *Canadian Composer* said: 'Quebec's entire cultural scene has been affected by playwright – and lyricist – Michel Tremblay. He is certainly the most important figure in Quebec theatre.' He is a great populist, always ready to take part in TV chat shows or be the willing subject of newspaper articles. He is a household name in Quebec, his popularity on a scale that playwrights such as Ayckbourn or Pinter have achieved in England. Nor has this celebrity dimmed with time. In 1988 *Saturday Night* described Tremblay's importance to Quebec as follows: 'At its best, Quebec theatre unites on stage the worlds of high art and outrageous theatricality in a synthesis very few other cultures have achieved in this century. A good measure of the credit must go to Michel Tremblay and to the success and scandal of *Les Belles-Soeurs* . . . Tremblay is the reigning literary figure of his generation'.

Annika Bluhm
London, 1991

THE GUID SISTERS

Characters

GERMAINE LAUZON
LINDA LAUZON
ROSE OUIMET
GABRIELLE JODOIN
LISETTE DE COURVAL
MARIE-ANGE BROUILLETTE
YVETTE LONGPRE
DES-NEIGES VERRETTE
THERESE DUBUC
OLIVINE DUBUC
ANGELINE SAUVE
RHEAUNA BIBEAU
LISE PAQUETTE
GINETTE MENARD
PIERRETTE GUERIN

Setting

The play is set in the kitchen of a tenement flat. Four enormous boxes occupy the centre of the room.

The action takes place in 1965 in Montreal.

This text is the version used in performance by the Tron Theatre Company.

The Guid Sisters was first performed in Great Britain at the Tron Theatre, Glasgow, on 2 May 1989. The cast was as follows:

GERMAINE LAUZON	Una McLean
LINDA LAUZON	Maureen Carr
ROSE OUIMET	Myra McFadyen
GABRIELLE JODOIN	Ann Louise Ross
LISETTE DE COURVAL	Elaine Collins
MARIE-ANGE BROUILLETTE	Donalda Samuel
YVETTE LONGPRE	Gaylie Runciman
DES-NEIGES VERRETTE	Jannette Foggo
THERESE DUBUC	Anne Lacey
OLIVINE DUBUC	Primrose Milligan
ANGELINE SAUVE	Irene Sunters
RHEAUNA BIBEAU	Kay Gallie
LISE PAQUETTE	Jenny McCrindle
GINETTE MENARD	Ali Ponta
PIERRETTE GUERIN	Muriel Romanes

Directed by Michael Boyd
Designed by Marek Obtulowicz & Michael Boyd
Costume Design Marion Thomson
Lighting Design Nick McCall
Stage Manager Jo Masson
Translated by Bill Findlay & Martin Bowman

The Guid Sisters was revived by the Tron Theatre Company for the 1990 Mayfest and opened at The Clyde Theatre, Glasgow, on 29 May 1990. In June 1990 it then played the World Stage Festival of International Theatre, Toronto, Canada.

There were the following changes in the cast:

GERMAINE LAUZON	Elaine C. Smith
THERESE DUBUC	Jo Cameron Brown
RHEAUNA BIBEAU	Ann Scott Jones

Designed by Kenny Miller
Lighting Design Colin Salter

ACT ONE

Linda enters. She notices the four boxes placed in the middle of the room.

LINDA. In the name ae God! What's all this? Maw!

GERMAINE (*in another room*). Is that you, Linda?

LINDA. Aye! What's gaun on? The kitchen's stowed wi boxes.

GERMAINE. They're ma stamps.

LINDA. What? They've come already? Here, that was fast work.

GERMAINE *enters*.

GERMAINE. Aye, it surprised me an all. Jist after ye went oot this mornin the doorbell went an when I goes tae answer it here's this big fellie. Aw, you'da liked him, Linda. Jist your type. Aboot twenty-two, twenty-three mebbe. Dark curly hair. Dinky wee moustache, ye know. Really good-lookin. He says tae me, 'Are you the lady of the house, Mme. Germaine Lauzon?' I says, 'Yes, that's myself.' And he says, 'Splendid, I've brought you your stamps.' I was that excited I didnae know what tae say. Then two fellies started carryin in the boxes intae the hoose an this other one's gien me this big fancy speech. Aw, he was a beautiful talker, an nice wi it tae, know what I mean? You'da liked him awright, Linda.

LINDA. Aw, get on wi it. What did he say?

GERMAINE. I cannae mind. I was owre excited. I think he said somethin aboot the company he works for and how pleased they were I'd won a million premium stamps . . . an that I was very lucky . . . Me, I couldnae find ma tongue. I wish your father'd been here. He'da kent what tae say tae him. I'm no sure if I even thanked him . . .

LINDA. That's gaunnae be a hoor ae a lot ae stamps tae lick. Four boxes! A mull-yin stamps! That's serious.

GERMAINE. Only three ae them's got stamps. The other one's

the books. But, listen, I had an idea, Linda. Ye'll no have tae stick them all yoursel. Are ye gaun oot the night?

LINDA. Aye, Robert's supposed tae be phonin me.

GERMAINE. Why no go oot the morra's night? See, I had this idea. I've phoned all ma sisters, an your father's sister, an I've been tae see the neighbours. I've invited them all tae a stamp-stickin party the night. Is that no a good idea? I've bought some sweeties an monkey-nuts an I've sent the wean tae get some Coke . . .

LINDA. Aw, maw! Ye know fine I aye go oot on Thursday night. It's me an Robert's night oot. We're gaunnae go tae the pictures.

GERMAINE. Ye cannae go oot an leave me on a night like this. I've got aboot fifteen folk comin . . .

LINDA. Are ye off your heid? Fifteen folk in this kitchen? An ye know fine we cannae use the rest ae the hoose for the painters are in. Jesus, maw! Sometimes you're really widden.

GERMAINE. That's right. Put me doon as usual. Okay-dokay, Linda, jist you carry on. Please yoursel. That's all ye ever dae anyway. It's nothin new. What a bloody life. I can never hae a bit a bloody pleasure for masel. Some bugger's aye got tae spoil it for me. But you go tae the pictures, Linda. Jist you carry on. If that's what ye want, suit yoursel. Christ-All-Bloody-Mighty!

LINDA. Aw, come on, mum, try tae understand.

GERMAINE. I dinnae want tae understand. I dinnae want tae even hear aboot it. Ye caw yir pan oot bringin them up an what dae ye get? Damn all! Jist sweet bugger all! An you cannae even dae me a wee favour. I'm warnin you, Linda. I've had it up tae here wi servin you hand and foot. You an the rest ae them. I'm no a skivvie, ye know. I've got a mullyin stamps tae stick an if you think I'm gaunnae dae it all masel, you've got another thought comin. An what's more, thae stamps are for the whole family, sae yese have all got tae dae your share. Your father's on the night-shift but that didnae stop him fae offerin tae help the morra if we dinnae get finished the night. I'm no askin for the moon. Why d'ye no help me for once instead ae wastin your time on that waster?

LINDA. Robert's no a waster. Jist gie it a break.

GERMAINE. Noo I've heard it all. Christ, I kent you were stupid, but no that stupid. When are you gaunnae realise that your nice Robert's jist a lazy gett? He disnae even make 60 bucks a week. The best he can manage is tae take ye tae the pictures once a week – an on a Thursday at that. I'm tellin you, Linda. Take your mother's advice. Keep hangin around wi that waster an ye'll end up jist like him. D'ye want tae marry a helpless gett an go round wipin his arse for him all your life?

LINDA. Aw, shut your mouth, mum. Ye don't know what you're talkin aboot. Jist drop it . . . I'll stay in the night . . . jist stop yappin on aboot it, right? An for your information, Robert's due a rise in a wee while an he'll be coinin it in then. He's no as useless as you think. His gaffer tellt me himsel that Robert'll be in the big money in nae time an they'll be makin him an under-gaffer. You wait, 80 bucks a week is nothin tae sniff at. Anyway . . . I'm gaunnae phone him an tell him I cannae make it tae the pictures the night . . . Hey, why dae I no tell him tae come round an stick stamps wi us?

GERMAINE. For-crying-oot-loud, I've jist stood here an tellt ye I cannae stomach him an ye ask me if ye can bring him here the night. Have ye nae heid on your shoulders, lassie? What did I dae tae the Good Lord in Heaven tae deserve such eejits? Jist this afternoon I asked your wee brother tae get me a bag ae tatties an he comes hame with a bottle ae milk. I dinnae understand it! I have tae repeat everythin twenty bloody times! Nae wonder I lose ma rag. I tellt ye, Linda. This party's for females. Jist fee-males. Your Robert's no poofie, is he?

LINDA. Awright, awright, don't go off the deep-end. I'll tell him no tae come. Jesus, ye cannae dae a bloody thing right around here. D'ye think I feel like stickin stamps after bein at ma work all day? . . . Why d'ye no go an dae some dustin in the livin-room, eh?

GERMAINE *goes out.* LINDA *dials a telephone number.*

Ye don't have tae listen tae what I'm gaunnae say . . . Hello, is Robert there? . . . When do you expect him? . . . Fine, then. Will you tell him that Linda phoned . . . I'm just fine, Mme. Bergeron. How're you? . . . That's great . . . Right-o, then. Thanks very much. Cheerio.

She hangs up. The telephone rings immediately.

Hullo? . . . Maw, you're wanted on the phone.

GERMAINE (*entering*). Twenty years ae age an ye still don't know tae say, 'Just one moment, please'.

LINDA. It's only Auntie Rose. I don't see why I should be polite tae her.

GERMAINE (*covering the receiver with her hand*). Wheesht! D'ye want her tae hear ye?

LINDA. Away an shite!

GERMAINE *looks out the window across the alley.*

GERMAINE. Hello? Oh, it's you, Rose . . . Aye, they've come. What dae ye think ae that, eh? A mull-yin stamps! They're sittin right here in front ae me but I still cannae take it in. A mull-yin ae them. I cannae even count that far but I know it's a hoor ae a lot. Aye, they sent a catalogue. I already had last year's, but this one's for this year so it's a lot better . . . The auld one was fallin apart anyway . . . Wait till ye see the lovely stuff they've got. Ye'll no credit it. I think I'll can get the whole jingbang an refurnish the hoose fae top tae bottom. I'm gaunnae get a new cooker, a new fridge, an new kitchen units. I think I'll get the red ones wi the gold trim. Ye'll no have saw thae yins, will ye? . . . Aw, they're that nice. I'm gaunnae get new pans, new cutlery, a full set ae dishes, a cruet set. Oh, an ye know thae cut glass crystal tumblers wi the 'caprice' design? Ye know how beautiful they are. Mme. de Courval got a set last year. She bummed that she paid a fortune for them, but I'm gettin mines for nothin. She'll no half be fizzin, eh? . . . What? . . . Aye, she'll be here the night, tae. They've got thae shiny chromium canisters for salt, pepper, tea, coffee, sugar, the whole lot. I'm getting them all . . . I'm gettin a colonial style bedroom suite wi all the accessories. There's curtains, dressin-table covers, one ae thae rugs ye put on the floor aside the bed, new wallpaper . . . Naw, no the one wi the floral pattern. It'd gie Henri a sore heid when he went tae his bed . . . I'm tellin ye, ma bedroom's gaunnae be really bee-yootiful. An for the livin-room I'm gettin a complete stereo unit, a big colour TV, a synthetic nylon carpet, an pictures . . . Ye know thae Chinese ones done in the velvet? . . . Aren't they jist? But hold on till ye hear this . . . I'm gaunnae get the same set ae crystal vases as your guid-sister, Aline! I wouldnae like tae say, but I think mines are even lovelier. I'm gaunnae be that chuffed! I think the livin-room'll be fair smashin, eh? . . . There's an electric razor for Henri, shower curtains . . . So what? We'll have one put in. It all

comes wi the stamps. There's a sunken bath, a new wash-hand
basin, swimsuits for everybody . . . Naw, Rose. Ma arse is no
too big. Dinnae act it. I'm gaunnae have the wean's bedroom
redone. Have ye seen what they've got for weans' bedrooms?
Rose, it's oot this world! They've got Mickey Mouse runnin
owre everything. An for Linda's room . . . Eh? Aye, awright,
ye'll can see it in the catalogue. Come across the noo though,
for the others'll be here any minute. I tellt them for tae come
early. It's gaunnae take till doomsday tae stick all thir stamps.

MARIE-ANGE *enters.*

Awright, I've got tae go. Mme. Brouillette's jist come in. Okay-
doke, aye . . . right, Cheerio!

MARIE-ANGE. I cannae hide it fae ye, Mme. Lauzon. I'm awfie
jealous.

GERMAINE. Well, I know how ye feel. It's a right turn up for the
books, right enough. Will ye excuse me for a minute, Mme.
Brouillette? I'm no jist ready. I was speakin tae ma sister, Rose.
I was lookin at her through the window. Ye know how we can
see one another across the alley. It's awfie handy that.

MARIE-ANGE. Is she comin tae?

GERMAINE. Oh aye. She wouldnae miss this for love nor
money. Here, have a seat. While you're waitin ye can have a
look at the catalogue. Wait till ye see the beautiful things
they've got. I'm gaunnae get everything. Everything. The whole
catalogue.

GERMAINE *goes into her bedroom.*

MARIE-ANGE. You'll no catch me winnin somethin like thon.
Nae danger. I bide in a shit-hoose an that's where I'll be till the
day I die. A mull-yin stamps! Thon's a whole hooseful. If I
dinnae stop thinkin aboot it I'm gaunnae go off ma skull. It's
ayeways the way. The ones wi all the luck are the ones 'at least
deserves it. What's thon Mme. Lauzon ever done tae deserve all
this? Nothin! No a bloody thing! She's nae better-lookin nor
me. In fact, she's nae better full-stop. Thae competitions
shouldnae be allowed. The priest was right the other day. They
should be abolished. Why should she win a mullyin stamps an
no me? Why? It's no fair. I've got weans tae keep clean tae, and
I work as hard as she does, wipin their arses mornin, noon an
night. In fact, ma weans are a damnsight cleaner nor hers. Why

d'ye think I'm all skin an bone? Cause I work ma guts oot, that's why. But look at her. She's as fat as a pig. And noo I've got tae live ben the waw fae her an her beautiful, free hoose. I tell ye, it makes me boke. It really makes me boke. No jist that, I'll have tae put up with her bummin her load. She's jist the type, the big-heided bitch. It's all I'll be hearin fae noo on. Nae wonder I'm scunnert. I'm no gaunnae spend ma life in this shite-hole while Lady Muck here plays the madam. It's no fair. I'm scunnert sweatin ma guts oot for nothin. Ma life is nothin. Nothin. I havnae got two cents tae rub thegither. I'm sick tae death ae this empty, scunnerin life. ⇑

During this monologue GABRIELLE, ROSE, YVETTE *and* LISETTE *have made their entry. They have sat down in the kitchen without paying attention to* MARIE-ANGE. *The five women stand up and turn towards the audience. The lighting changes.*

THE FIVE WOMEN (*together*). This empty, scunnerin life! Monday!

LISETTE. When the sun has begun to caress with its rays the wee flowers in the fields and the wee birds have opened wide their wee beaks to offer up to heaven their wee prayers . . .

THE OTHERS. I drag masel up for tae make the breakfast. Coffee, toast, ham an eggs. I'm vernear demented jist gettin the rest ae them up oot their stinkers. The weans leave for the school. Ma man goes tae his work.

MARIE-ANGE. No mine. He's on the dole. He stays in his pit.

THE FIVE WOMEN. Then I works like a daft yin till one o'clock. I wash shirts, socks, jerseys, underclaes, bras, breeks, skirts, frocks . . . The whole lot. I scrub them. I rinse them. I wring them oot. Ma hands are red raw. Ma back is stoonin. At one o'clock the weans come hame. They eat like pigs. They turn the hoose upside doon. Then they clear oot. In the afternoon I hang oot the washin. It's the worst. I hate it. After that, I make the tea. They all come hame. They're crabbit. There's aye a rammy. Then at night we watch the telly. Tuesday.

LISETTE. When the sun has begun to caress with its rays the wee flowers in the fields and the wee birds have opened wide their wee beaks . . .

THE OTHERS. I drag masel up for tae make the breakfast. Ayeways the same bloody thing. Coffee, toast, ham an eggs. I pull them oot their beds an hunt them oot the door. Then it's the ironin. I work, I work, an I work. It's one o'clock afore I know where I am an the weans are bawlin for their dinner isnae ready. I open a tin ae luncheon meat an make pieces. I work all afternoon. Tea-time comes. There's aye a rammy. Then at night we watch the telly. Wednesday . . . Message day. I'm on ma feet all day. I break ma back humphin bags ae messages. I gets hame deadbeat but I've got tae make the tea. When the rest get hame I'm washed oot. Ma man starts cursin. The weans start bawlin. Then at night we watch the telly. Thursday, then Friday . . . It's the same thing. I slave. I skivvy. I caw ma guts oot for a pack ae getts. Then Saturday, tae cap it all, I've got the weans on ma back all day. Then at night we watch the telly. Sunday we go on the bus for tea at the mother-in-law's. I have tae watch the weans like a hawk. I have tae kid on I'm laughin at the father-in-law's jokes. Ha-bloody-ha! I have tae no choke on the auld bitch's cookin. They aye rub in ma face that hers's better'n mines. Then, at night, we watch the telly. I'm sick ae this empty, scunnerin life! This empty, scunnerin life! This empty. . .

The lighting returns to normal. They sit down abruptly.

LISETTE. When I was in Europe . . .

ROSE. There she goes on aboot her bloody Europe again. Get her gaun on that an she'll be at it all night.

DES-NEIGES *comes in. Discreet little greetings.*

LISETTE. I was only wanting to say that they don't have stamps in Europe. Well, they have stamps, but not this kind. Just the kind you put on letters.

DES-NEIGES. Ye mean ye cannae win presents like here? That Europe disnae sound like much ae a place.

LISETTE. Oh no, it's a very nice place just the same . . .

MARIE-ANGE. I'm no against stamps, mind you. They're awfie handy. If it werenae for the stamps I'd still be waitin for ma mincer. What I've nae time for is thae competitions.

LISETTE. But why? They can bring so much pleasure to the whole family.

MARIE-ANGE. Aye, mebbe. But they're a pain in the arse for the folk next door.

LISETTE. Really, Mme. Brouillette! There's no need for that foul language. You never hear me stooping to that to say what I want.

MARIE-ANGE. I'll talk the way I want an I'll say jist what I want tae say! Right! I've never been tae your Europe – I wouldnae want tae turn pan-loaf an mealy-mouthed like you.

ROSE. Hey, youse two, dinnae start. We didnae come here tae argybargy. If yese keep at it I'm gaun oot that door, doon thae stairs, and hame.

GABRIELLE. Why's Germaine takin sae long? Germaine!

GERMAINE (*in her bedroom*). I'll no be long. I'm havin trouble wi . . . Oh, bugger it! Linda, are you there?

GABRIELLE. Linda! Linda! Naw, she's no here.

MARIE-ANGE. I think I seen her go oot a while back.

GERMAINE. Dinnae tell me she's sneaked oot, the wee bitch.

GABRIELLE. Can we start stickin the stamps while we're waitin for ye?

GERMAINE. Naw, hold on! I'll have tae show yese what yese've got tae dae. Dinnae start athoot me. Wait till I come. Jist have a wee blether for a minute.

GABRIELLE. 'Have a wee blether for a minute'? What are we gaunnae blether aboot?

The telephone rings.

ROSE. Jesus Christ, that gien me a fright! Hullo! Naw, she's oot. But if ye want tae hold on she'll no be long. She'll be back in a minute.

She puts down the receiver, goes out on the balcony and shouts.

Linda! Linda! Telephone.

LISETTE. So tell me, Mme. Longpré, how is your daughter Claudette enjoying married life?

YVETTE. Oh, she likes it jist fine. She's fair enjoyin hersel. She had a rare honeymoon, she tellt me.

GABRIELLE. Where did they go tae?

YVETTE. Well, her man won a competition for a holiday in the

Canary Islands, so they had tae bring the weddin forward a bit . . .

ROSE (*laughing*). The Canary Islands! That'd be jist the place for a honeymoon. The cocks sit on the nest all day there.

GABRIELLE. Settle doon, Rose!

ROSE. What's wrong?

DES-NEIGES. The Canary Islands, where aboots are they?

LISETTE. My husband and I stopped off there on our last trip to Europe. It's an awfie . . . It's an awfully nice country. Do you know, the women wear nothing but grass skirts.

ROSE. Ma man would love that!

LISETTE. Mind you, the people there don't believe in keeping themselves very clean. It's the same in Europe. They don't go in for washing much either.

DES-NEIGES. It shows an all. Look at thon Italian woman next door tae me. Ye wouldnae credit the guff comes off yon woman.

The women burst out laughing.

LISETTE (*insinuating*). Have you ever happened to notice her washing-line on a Monday?

DES-NEIGES. No, why?

LISETTE. Well, I'll say no more than this . . . nobody in that family ever wears underwear.

MARIE-ANGE. Ach away! I dinnae believe it!

YVETTE. You're kiddin us on.

LISETTE. It's as true as I'm sittin here! Just you look for yourselves next Monday. Then you'll see.

YVETTE. Nae wonder they stink.

MARIE-ANGE. Mebbe she's sae shy she hangs them inside.

All the others laugh.

LISETTE. Shy? A European? They don't know the meaning of the word. You only have to look at their films on the television to see that. They're disgusting. People kissing in broad daylight! It's in their blood, of course. They're born like that. You only

have to watch that Italian's daughter when her friends come
round . . . her boyfriends, that is. It's a downright disgrace
what she gets up to, that girl. She's got no shame! Oh, that
reminds me, Mme. Ouimet, I saw your Michel the other day . . .

ROSE. No wi that wee hoor!

LISETTE. I'm sorry it's me that has to tell you, but yes.

ROSE. Ye must've made a mistake. It couldnae have been ma
Michel.

LISETTE. Well, the Italians are my neighbours, too, you know.
The two of them were out on the front balcony. I suppose they
didn't think anyone could see them.

DES-NEIGES. It's right enough, Mme. Ouimet. I saw them an all.
They were all owre each other, kissin an cuddlin.

ROSE. The wee bugger! As if one sex-mad gett in the family
wasnae enough. His father cannae even see a bint on the telly
athoot gettin a hard-on! Bloody sex! They never can get
enough, thae Ouimets. They're all the same in that family.
They . . .

GABRIELLE. Rose, ye dinnae have tae broadcast it tae the whole
world . . .

LISETTE. But we're very interested . . .

DES-NEIGES & MARIE-ANGE. Aye, so we are. . . .

YVETTE. Tae get back tae ma lassie's honeymoon . . .

GERMAINE *enters, all dressed up.*

GERMAINE. Here I am, girls!

Greetings, 'Hullos', 'How are yese', etc.

Well, what've yese all been bletherin aboot?

ROSE. Mme. Longpré was tellin us all aboot her Claudette's
honeymoon.

GERMAINE. Get away! Hullo, Madame. An what was she sayin?

ROSE. They seem tae have had a really nice time. They met all
kinna folk. They went tae the Canary Islands. They went oot in
a boat. They went fishin. They catched fish this big. They ran
intae some other couples they knew . . . some friends ae

Claudette's. They all came hame thegither. They stopped off in
New York. Mme. Longpré has jist been tellin us all aboot it . . .

YVETTE. Well . . .

ROSE. Is that no right, Mme. Longpré, eh?

YVETTE. Well, aye, but . . .

GERMAINE. You mind an tell your lassie, Mme. Longpré, that I
wish her all future happiness. We werenae invited tae the
weddin right enough, but we wish her all the best jist the same.

Embarrassed silence.

GABRIELLE. Hey! It's comin up for seven o'clock! The rosary!

GERMAINE. Oh help-ma-Christ, ma novena for Saint Thérèse!
I'll go an get Linda's transistor.

She goes out.

ROSE. What does she need Saint Thérèse for after winnin all
thon?

DES-NEIGES. Mebbe her kids are gien her a hard time ae it . . .

GABRIELLE. Naw, I dinnae think sae. She'd a tellt me . . .

GERMAINE (*in* LINDA's *bedroom*). Christ Almighty! Where's she
put the bloody thing?

ROSE. I'm no so sure, Gaby. Sometimes our sister's a bit secret-
like.

GABRIELLE. No wi me she isnae. She tells me everythin. You,
you're owre much ae a gossip . . .

ROSE. What dae ye mean, 'gossip'? You can fine talk. Ma
mouth's naewhere near as big as yours, Gabrielle Jodoin.

GABRIELLE. Aw, come off it. Ye know damn fine ye cannae keep
anythin tae yoursel.

ROSE. If you think for one minute . . .

LISETTE. Now, now, Mme. Ouimet. Weren't you just saying a
wee while ago that we didn't come here to argue?

ROSE. You away an shite in your ain midden. An for your
information, I didnae say 'argue', I said 'argybargy'.

GERMAINE *comes back in with her radio.*

GERMAINE. What's gaun on? I can hear yese bawlin fae the other end ae the hoose!

GABRIELLE. Och, it's that sister ae oors at it again . . .

GERMAINE. Jist settle doon, Rose, eh! Jist don't start any argybargyin the night.

ROSE. Ye see! In oor family we say 'argybargyin'.

GERMAINE *turns on the radio. We hear strains of the rosary being said. All the women kneel. After five or six 'Hail Marys' a great commotion is heard outside. All the women scream, get up and rush out.*

GERMAINE. Oh ma God! It's ma guid-sister, Thérèse. Her mother-in-law's jist fell doon three sets ae stairs.

ROSE. Did ye hurt yoursel, Mme. Dubuc?

GABRIELLE. Rose, shut your mouth! She must be half-deid!

THERESE (*from a distance*). Are ye awright, Mme. Dubuc? (*We hear an indistinct moan.*) Jist hold on a minute. Let me get the wheelchair off ye. Is that better? I'm gaunnae help ye get back intae your chair noo. Come on, Mme. Dubuc, jist make a wee bit ae effort. Dinnae jist let yoursel hang like that. Come on, pull yoursel up.

DES-NEIGES. I'll come doon an gie ye a hand.

THERESE. Thanks, Mlle. Verrette. It's very good ae ye.

The other women re-enter the room.

ROSE. Germaine, switch off that wireless. I'm a bag ae nerves.

GERMAINE. What aboot ma novena?

ROSE. How far did ye get?

GERMAINE. Up tae seven. But I promised I'd dae nine.

ROSE. Seven days? So what? Ye can start again the morra an ye'll be finished your nine next Saturday.

GERMAINE. Ma novena's no for nine days. It's for nine weeks.

Enter THERESE, DES-NEIGES, *and* OLIVINE *in her wheelchair.*

GERMAINE. Oh my God, was she hurt bad?

THERESE. Naw, naw, she's used tae it. She falls oot her chair ten times a day. Whew! I've nae breath left. It's nae joke humphin

that contraption up three flights ae stairs. D'ye think I could
have a drink, Germaine?

GERMAINE. Gaby, gie Thérèse a glass ae water.

She approaches OLIVINE.

How are ye the day, Mme. Dubuc?

THERESE. Dinnae get owre close, Germaine. She's started bitin
noo.

OLIVINE *tries to bite* GERMAINE's *hand.*

GERMAINE. By the Christ, you're right! She's dangerous! How
long's she been daein that?

THERESE. Would ye mind turnin off the wireless, Germaine? Ma
heid's birlin. Ma nerves are shot tae hell after that carry-on.

GERMAINE *reluctantly turns off the radio.*

GERMAINE. Not at all, Thérèse, hen. I know how ye feel, ye
poor thing ye.

THERESE. I've had as much as I can take. Ye've nae idea the life
I lead havin her on ma back all the time. It's no that I'm no
fond ae her, the poor auld soul. Ye cannae help but feel sorry
for her. But ye never know when she's gaunnae take one ae her
turns. I've got tae keep ma eye on her mornin, noon an night.

DES-NEIGES. How come she's oot the hospital?

THERESE. Well, ye see, Mlle. Verrette, three months ago ma man
got a rise, so the welfare stopped payin for his mother. If
she'da stayed there, we'd've had tae pay all the hospital bills
oursels.

MARIE-ANGE. Dearie-mearie . . .

YVETTE. That's awfie . . .

DES-NEIGES. What a shame.

During THERESE's *speech,* GERMAINE *opens the boxes and
distributes the booklets and stamps.*

THERESE. We had tae take her oot. We had nae choice. An ye
can take it fae me that she's a real handful. Ye expect nae better
at ninety-three, but it's like lookin after a wean. I've got tae
dress her, wash her, undress her. . .

DES-NEIGES. My, my!

YVETTE. Ye poor thing right enough.

THERESE. It's nae joke I can tell ye. Jist this mornin, for instance, I said tae Paolo, ma youngest, 'Your mummy's gaun her messages, so you stay here an look after your granny.' Ye wouldnae credit it. When I got back the auld yin had poured a tin ae syrup all owre hersel an was plooterin in it like a daftie. Of course, Paolo was naewhere tae be seen. I had tae wash doon the table, the floor, the wheelchair . . .

GERMAINE. What aboot Mme. Dubuc?

THERESE. I jist left her the way she was for the rest ae the afternoon tae learn her. If she's gaun tae act like a wean, I'm gaunnae treat her like one. Would ye credit that I've even got tae spoonfeed her?

GERMAINE. Aw, poor Thérèse. Ma heart goes oot tae ye, doll.

DES-NEIGES. You're too good, Thérèse.

GABRIELLE. Aye. Far too good.

THERESE. Well, we've all got our crosses tae bear.

MARIE-ANGE. If ye ask me, Thérèse, yours's got skelves!

THERESE. Ach well, I dinnae complain. I jist tell masel that the Lord is Good and He'll help me get by.

LISETTE. I think I'm going to cry.

THERESE. Noo, noo, Mme. de Courval, dinnae upset yoursel.

DES-NEIGES. All I can say, Mme. Dubuc, is I think you're a saint.

GERMAINE. Right then. Noo that yese've all got stamps and books, I'll put a wee drop water in some saucers an we can get started, eh? Ye're no here tae spend the whole night bletherin.

She fills a few saucers with water and hands them around. The women begin pasting the stamps.

If Linda's oot there, she can come in an gie's a hand.

She goes out on the balcony.

Linda! Linda! Richard, have ye seen oor Linda? . . . Aw, in the name ae . . . She's got some cheek gallivantin tae that cafe while

I'm cawin ma pan oot here. Be a good laddie and go an tell her
tae get right hame pronto. An you come and see Mme. Lauzon
the morra, son. She'll gie ye some sweeties if there's any left,
okay? Away ye go then, son, an tell her she's tae come hame
right this minute.

She comes back inside.

The wee gett. She promised me she'd stay in the hoose.

MARIE-ANGE. Young yins are all the same.

THERESE. Aye, they're all the same. They only think ae theirsels.

GABRIELLE. Oh wheesht, ye neednae tell me aboot it. I've got
ma hands full at hame. Ever since he went tae that university
ma Raymond's changed somethin terrible. Ye wouldnae
recognise him. He walks around wi his nose in the air as if he
was owre guid for the likes ae us, blethers away in Latin most
ae the time, an makes us listen tae that daft bloody music ae
his. Would ye credit it, classical music – an in the middle ae the
afternoon at that. An if we dinnae want tae watch his stupid
television programmes, he throws a fit. If there's one thing I
cannae stand, it's classical bloody music.

ROSE. You're no the only one.

THERESE. I cannae stand it neither. It gie's me a sore heid.
Bang-bang here, an boom-booms there.

GABRIELLE. Of course, Raymond says we dinnae understand it.
It beats me that there's anything tae understand. Jist cause he's
learnin all kinna stupid nonsense at that university, he thinks
we're no good enough for him. I've got a guid mind tae stop
his money.

ALL THE WOMEN. Kids are that ungrateful! Kids are that
ungrateful!

GERMAINE. Mind an fill the books up, eh? Nae empty pages.

ROSE. Awright, Germaine, awright. We know how tae dae it. It's
no the first time we've stuck stamps.

YVETTE. D'ye no think it's gettin a bit warm in here? Could we
no open the window a wee bit?

GERMAINE. Naw, naw. It'll cause a draught. I'm feart for ma
stamps.

ROSE. Aw, come on, Germaine. They're no canaries. They'll no
fly away. That reminds me, talkin ae canaries, last Sunday past I
went tae see Bernard, ma auldest boy. I've never seen that
many birds in the one hoose. The place was hoatchin wi them.
That hoose is more like a big doocot. An it's all her daein.
She's bird-daft. She'll no get rid ae any of them for she says
she's owre soft-hearted. Well, fair's fair, mebbe she is soft-
hearted, but surely tae God there's a limit. Listen till yese hear
this. It'll kill yese.

Spotlight on ROSE.

Last Easter, Bernard picked up this bird cage for the two weans.
Some fellie doon at the bar was needin money, so he selled it
cheap wi the birds in it an everythin . . . Well, the minute her
nibs saw the cage an the birds, she went the craw road. She fell
in love wi thae wee birds. She looked after them better than she
looked after her ain weans. I'm no exaggeratin. An of course
afore ye knew it the females started layin eggs . . . An when the
eggs hatched, she thought they were jist her wee darlins. I'd've
flushed them doon the lavvy.

She bursts out laughing. The lighting returns to normal.

YVETTE. Is she no a scream! There's nae holding her doon. Ye
can aye depend on her for a laugh.

GABRIELLE. Aye, Rose is aye the heart and soul ae a party.

ROSE. Well, ma motto is when it's time tae have a laugh, ye
might as well pish yoursel. Even the sad ones I tell come oot
comical.

THERESE. You're gey lucky you can say that, Mme. Ouimet. It's
no everybody . . .

DES-NEIGES. We understand, hen. It must be hard for ye tae
laugh wi all your problems. You're far owre good, Mme.
Dubuc. You're aye thinkin ae other folk . . .

ROSE. That's right. Ye should think aboot yoursel sometimes,
Mme. Dubuc. Ye never go oot.

THERESE. I don't have the time! When can ye see me gettin oot?
I havnae the time. I've got tae look after her . . . And even if
there was nothin else. . .

GERMAINE. How d'ye mean? Dinnae tell me there's somethin
else, Thérèse.

THERESE. Ye don't know the half ae it. Noo that ma man's got a rise, the family thinks we're rollin in it. Jist yesterday ma guid-sister's guid-sister came tae the hoose moochin. Well, ye know me. When she gien me her sob story ma heart jist went oot tae her. So I gien her some auld claes I didnae need any more . . . Oh, she was that pleased . . . She started greetin . . . She even tried tae kiss ma hands.

DES-NEIGES. I'm no surprised. Ye deserved it.

MARIE-ANGE. I really think you're an angel, Mme. Dubuc.

THERESE. Och, dinnae say that . . .

DES-NEIGES. Oh but aye. It's true. That's jist what ye are. A pure angel.

LISETTE. It certainly is, Mme. Dubuc. We greatly admire you. And you can be sure I won't forget you in my prayers.

THERESE. Well, I aye say tae masel, 'If God has put poor folk on this earth, they've got tae be helped.'

GERMAINE. Hey, I've an idea. When ye've finished fillin up your books, intead ae pilin them up on the table, why dae we no put them back in the box? . . . Rose, gie me a hand . . . We'll skail all the empty books oot this box an fill it up wi the ones wi the stamps stuck in.

ROSE. Aye, that'd be more sensible. Help ma God! That's one hoor ae a lot ae books! We'll never full them all the night!

GERMAINE. Why can we no? Everybody's no here yet, mind, so we . . .

DES-NEIGES. Who else is comin, Mme. Lauzon?

GERMAINE. Rhéauna Bibeau and Angéline Sauvé said they'd cry in after they've been tae the chapel ae rest. One ae Mlle. Bibeau's friends has a lassie 'at's man's jist died. I think his name was Baril.

YVETTE. No Rosaire Baril?

GERMAINE. Aye, I think that's it.

YVETTE. Oh my God, I knew him well! Him an me were winshin at one time. My God, would ye imagine that. I'da been a widow the day.

GERMAINE. Hey, lassies, yese'll no credit this but ye know that

Spot-the-Mistake competition in the paper? Well, I found all the eight mistakes last week . . . It was the first time I'd managed it so I decided tae put in an entry . . .

YVETTE. Did ye win anythin?

GABRIELLE. Dae I look like somebody 'at's won anything?

THERESE. Aw, Germaine, what ye gaunnae dae wi all thir stamps?

GERMAINE. Did I no tell ye? I'm gaunnae dae the hoose oot fae top tae bottom. Jist a minute . . . Where did I put the catalogue? . . . Ah, here it is. See, look at all that, Thérèse. I'm gaunnae get all thae things for nothin.

THERESE. All that for nothin! That's no real. Ye mean it's no gaunnae cost ye a cent?

GERMAINE. Not a cent! Are thae competitions no jist magic!

LISETTE. That's not what Mme. Brouillette was saying just a wee while ago.

GERMAINE. How come?

MARIE-ANGE. Och, Mme. de Courval!

ROSE. Well, oot wi it, Mme. Brouillette. Dinnae be feart tae say what ye think. Ye were sayin a minute ago ye didnae like thae competitions 'cause only one family wins.

MARIE-ANGE. Well, it's true. As far as I'm concerned all thae competitions an lotteries are jist a racket. They're no fair. I'm all against them.

GERMAINE. That's jist because ye've never won nothin.

MARIE-ANGE. Mebbe so, but that disnae stop them no bein fair.

GERMAINE. How d'ye mean, no fair? You're jist jealous, that's all. Ye said as much yoursel, the minute ye set foot in here. Well, I've nae time for jealous folk, Mme. Brouillette. I cannae stomach them one bit. In fact, if ye really want tae know, they gie me the boke.

MARIE-ANGE. Well! If that's your attitude, I'm leavin.

GERMAINE. Oh, here . . . look . . . wait . . . jist hold on a minute. I'm sorry. I was a bit short wi ye. I'm all nerves the night. Ma tongue disnae know what it's sayin any more. We'll say nae more aboot it, awright? Ye've every right tae your ain opinions. Every right. Jist sit doon and keep pastin, okay?

ROSE. Our sister here's feart she loses one ae her workers.

GABRIELLE. Shut it, Rose. Mind your ain business. You're aye sticking your neb in where it disnae belong.

ROSE. What's got intae you, for Christ's sake? Can I no even open ma mouth? There's nae talkin tae you the night.

MARIE-ANGE. Awright, I'll stay. But I'm still against them.

From this point on MARIE-ANGE *will steal all the booklets she fills. The others will see what she's doing from the outset (except* GERMAINE *of course) and will decide to do as she does.*

LISETTE. I solved the mystery charade in Chatelaine last month . . . You know, Chatelaine, that woman's magazine . . . It was very easy . . . The first clue was 'part of an old-fashioned car' . . .

ROSE. Ye mean like a horn? Ma man must be auld-fashioned tae as he's got one atween his legs! He's aye tootin it at me, the horny gett!

LISETTE. So I thought to myself, let's see . . . an old-fashioned car . . . charabang . . . yes, charabang, that must be it . . .

ROSE. Aye, that must be it, for ye cannae have a bang athoot a horn!

LISETTE. So part of an old-fashioned car would be part of the word for an old-fashioned car, don't you see? So char is part of charabang . . ..

ROSE. Aye, but char is part ae chariot tae . . . Ye know, chariot, an auld-fashioned car . . . the kind used for Roman in the gloamin . . . Dae yese no get it? Chariot. Roman in the gloamin . . . See, am I no good at thae word games?

LISETTE. The second clue was 'helpful' . . .

ROSE. That's what ma man says I am. Helpful. Every night in bed he says tae me, 'Could ye help me on, hen?' . . .

LISETTE. So I thought, help . . . helpful . . . assistance . . . to give a hand . . .

ROSE. Aye, that's exactly what I dae . . . Gie him a hand on . . .

LISETTE. Helpful . . . to give aid . . . aid . . . yes, that must be it, I thought, aid . . . because the mystery word meant a game played by society people . . .

ROSE. Mono-poly. (ROSE *pronounces the word in this distorted way*.)

GABRIELLE. Mono-poly?

ROSE. Aye, ye know, that game where the rich buy up everythin an rook the rest ae us . . .

GABRIELLE. Mono-poly? . . . Aw, Monopoly! . . . Noo I get it!

ROSE. An it's no often you get it . . .

GABRIELLE. Shut up Rose! . . . You know nothin. Tae think society folk would play Monopoly! (*To* LISETTE.) Would it be dominoes?

LISETTE. It's very easy really . . . char and aid . . . You see, it's not difficult if you know how . . . charade . . . Charade!

YVETTE. Charade? What's a charade?

LISETTE. I worked out what it was right away . . . It's simple when you know how . . .

YVETTE. Did ye win anythin?

LISETTE. Look! I didn't send in my answer. I don't need to resort to that sort of thing. I just did it for the challenge. Do I look like somebody needs to win prizes?

ROSE. For masel, I'm a dab hand at thae word competitions ye get in the papers. I've jist got tae see one an that's me away. Mystery words, crosswords, conundrums, anagrams, acrostics, riddle-me-rees, cryptograms, you name it an I've done it. Word-puzzles are ma speciality, be it scrambled words, back-tae-front words, upside-doon words, ootside-in words. I send ma answers all owre the place athoot fail. It costs me two dollar a week jist in stamps.

YVETTE. Have ye won anythin?

ROSE (*looking towards* GERMAINE). Dae I look like somedy 'at's won anythin?

THERESE. Mme. Dubuc, will ye please leave go ma saucer? Look! Noo ye've done it. Ye've spilled the whole lot! I've had it up tae here wi ye. Ye've jist gaun beyond the score noo.

She strikes her mother-in-law on the head, and her mother-in-law calms down a little.

GABRIELLE. Jesus wept, ye dinnae stand any nonsense off her, dae ye? Are ye no feart ye'll dae her an injury?

THERESE. Naw, naw. She's used tae it. It's the only way tae settle her doon. Ma man worked it oot. If ye gie her a guid skelp on the heid it seems tae quiet her doon for a while. That way there's no a cheep oot ae her an we get some peace.

Blackout.

Spotlight on YVETTE.

YVETTE. Ye can imagine how proud I was. When ma lassie Claudette got back fae her honeymoon, she gien me the top tier ae her weddin cake. Oh, it's that bonny. It's like a wee chapel all made oot ae icin. It's got a stair wi a wee red velvet runner on it that leads up tae a kinna stage, an on top ae the stage stands the bride an bridegroom. Two bonny wee dolls all dressed up jist like as if they'd jist got married. There's even a priest tae bless them, an at the back there's an altar. Ye wouldnae credit it was all done wi icin. It's really oot this world. Mind you, the cake didnae half cost us. It had six tiers! Of course, it wasnae all cake, though. Thon would a cost a fortune. Jist the top two tiers were cake. The rest was made ae wood. But ye could never a tellt. Anyways, ma lassie Claudette gien me the top tier as a mindin. She had it put in one ae thae glass bells for me so's tae preserve it. It looks that lovely, but I was feart it would turn foostie eventually, ye know, no gettin air. So I taen ma man's glass-cutter an cut oot a hole in the top ae the bell. Noo the air can get in tae circulate aboot the cake and it'll no go bad.

The lights come back on.

DES-NEIGES. I entered one ae thae word competitions no that long ago . . . Ye had tae find a slogan for a bookshop . . . ye know . . . that bookshop Hachette's . . . I worked quite a good one oot . . . 'Fill your ashet with books fae Hachette's!' That was quite good, eh?

YVETTE. Did you win anythin?

DES-NEIGES. Dae I look like somedy 'at's won anythin?

GERMAINE. Oh hear, Rose, I seen ye cuttin your grass this mornin. Ye should buy yoursel a mower.

ROSE. What for? I manage fine wi ma shears. Asides, it keeps me fit.

GERMAINE. Aw, who d'ye think your kiddin! Ye were pechin and blawin like an auld cart-horse.

ROSE. I'm tellin ye, I feel the better for it. Anyway, I cannae afford a mower. And even if I could, there's other things I'd rather spend ma money on.

GERMAINE. Well, see me, I'm gaunnae get a mower wi ma stamps . . .

DES-NEIGES. Her an her bloody stamps are beginnin tae get right up ma nose!

ROSE. What the hell are ye gaunnae dae wi a mower up on the third storey?

GERMAINE. Oh, ye never know, it might come in handy. And ye can never tell, we'll mebbe decide tae flit one ae these days.

DES-NEIGES. She'll be tellin us next she needs a new hoose tae put all the stuff in she gets wi her bloody stamps.

GERMAINE. And ye must admit, it looks like we'll need a bigger place for all the things I'll get wi ma stamps.

DES-NEIGES, MARIE-ANGE *and* THERESE *hide two or three booklets of stamps.*

Here, Rose, I'll lend ye ma new mower when I get it.

ROSE. Oh Christ, no! I'd mebbe break it. I'd be collectin stamps for the next two years jist tae pay ye back.

The women laugh.

GERMAINE. Ha, ha, ha. Dinnae be sae smart!

MARIE-ANGE. Is she no the limit! She takes some beatin that one!

THERESE. I worked oot the mystery voice competition on the wireless last week . . . It was an auld kinna voice . . . I recognised it was that politician Duplessis . . . It was ma man that twigged who it was first . . . I sent off twenty-five entries an jist for luck I put doon ma wee boy's name, Paolo Dubuc . . .

YVETTE. Did ye win anythin?

THERESE (*looking at* GERMAINE). Dae I look like somedy who's won anything?

GABRIELLE. Here, ye'll never guess what ma man's gaunnae buy me for ma birthday?

ROSE. Same as the year afore, I suppose. Two pairs ae nylons.

GABRIELLE. Funny bugger, eh. Naw, a fur coat. It's no real fur, of course, jist synthetic. But I dinnae think real fur's worth the money anymore anyhow. The artificial ones they make nooadays are jist as nice. In fact, sometimes they're nicer.

LISETTE. Oh, I can't agree with you there . . .

ROSE. Aw, here she starts. We all know who's got a big fat mink stole!

LISETTE. As far as I'm concerned there'll never be a substitute for real fur. By the by, did I tell you I'll be getting a new stole come the autumn? The one I have just now is three years old and it's starting to look . . . well, just a wee bit tired. Mind you, it's still quite presentable, but . . .

ROSE. Shut your big gob, ya bloody liar ye! We know damn fine your man's up tae his arse in debt acause ae your mink stoles an your fancy trips tae Europe. Ye cannae take us in wi all that shite aboot bein well-off. Ye've nae more money than the rest ae us. Christ, I've really had it up tae here wi that slaverin bitch bummin her load.

LISETTE. Mme. Jodoin, if your husband would be interested in buying my stole, I'd be prepared to part with it for a very reasonable price. That way you'd be sure of real mink. I always say that's what friends are for . . .

YVETTE. I sent in ma answers tae the 'Magnified Objects' competition . . . Ye know, the one where the pictures ae the objects are enlarged till they're that close up it's hard tae make oot what the objects are . . .

ROSE. If they're enlarged and hard, I know what they are . . .

YVETTE. Well, whatever, I identified them . . . The first was a screwdriver . . .

ROSE. Are ye sure it wasnae somethin else for screwin?

YVETTE. And the second was a hook.

THE OTHER WOMEN (*to* YVETTE). Did ye win anythin?

> YVETTE *contents herself with looking at* GERMAINE *and sitting down again.*

GERMAINE. Ye know Daniel, Mme. Robitaille's wee boy? He fell off the second floor balcony the other day. No even a scratch on him! What d'ye think ae that, eh?

MARIE-ANGE. Aye, an he landed on Mme. Dubé's hammock. And M. Dubé was havin a sleep in it at the time . . .

GERMAINE. That's right. M. Dubé's in the infirmary noo. He'll be in for three month.

DES-NEIGES. Talkin aboot accidents minds me ae a joke I heard the other day . . .

ROSE. Well, oot wi it then.

DES-NEIGES. Oh, I couldnae. It's too dirty . . .

ROSE. Aw come off it, Mlle. Verrette. It'll no be the first one ye've tellt us.

DES-NEIGES. I don't know how, but I'm a wee bit shy the night.

GABRIELLE. Stop actin it, Mlle. Verrette. Ye know damn fine ye're gauntae tell us anyway.

DES-NEIGES. Well . . . awright . . . here goes . . . There was this nun got raped up a passage.

ROSE. Front passage or back passage?

DES-NEIGES. And the next mornin they found her lyin on the ground in a back-court, all filthy dirty, wi her habit pulled back right up owre her heid. She was moanin away, no makin any sense. So this reporter comes up tae her and asks her 'Sister, could you give me some details about this terrible experience you've had?' She opens her eyes, smiles at him, and whispers 'Again. Again.'

> *All the women burst out laughing except for* LISETTE *who appears scandalised and* YVETTE *who does not get the joke.*

ROSE. Jesus wept, I'm gaunnae pish ma knickers. Where in hell d'ye find them, Mme. Verrette?

GABRIELLE. Oh, ye might well ask. Fae her travellin salesman.

DES-NEIGES. Mme. Jodoin! If ye don't mind.

ROSE. Oh aye, that's right enough. Her commercial traveller.

LISETTE. I don't understand.

GABRIELLE. Aye, Mlle. Verrette is friendly wi a travellin salesman 'at comes tae sell her brushes every month. Though if ye ask me, I think it's more nor his bristles she likes.

DES-NEIGES. Mme. Jodoin! Jist cut that oot!

ROSE. Well, I know one thing. Mlle. Verrette has more brushes in her hoose nor anybody else in the street . . . Hey, I seen your fancy man, the commercial traveller, the other day, Mme. Verrette. He was sittin in the cafe. He must've been up tae see ye, eh?

DES-NEIGES. Yes, he paid me a visit, but I can assure you that there's nothin atween me an him if that's what your insinuatin.

ROSE. That's what they all say.

DES-NEIGES. Mme. Ouimet! Sometimes I think your mind's twisted! You aye think the worst aboot folk. Monsieur Simard is a perfect gentleman.

ROSE. Well, we'll jist wait an see in nine months if you're as perfect. Noo, noo, calm doon, Mlle. Verrette, dinnae lose the rag. I'm jist windin ye up.

DES-NEIGES. An you know fine it upsets me when ye say things like that. I'm a respectable woman an a good Catholic. If ye must know, Henri . . . er . . . M. Simard came tae see me aboot a Party Plan idea he had. He wants me tae put on one ae thae hostess parties next week . . . in ma hoose. He's asked me tae invite all ae yese. He approached me as he knows ma hoose best . . . It'd be a week on Sunday, right after the chapel. I need at least ten folk tae come if I've tae get ma free gift . . . He gies away a set ae fancy cups tae the hostess for nothin. They're really beautiful cups. Really beautiful. Wi pictures ae the Niagara Falls on them. They're souvenirs he brought back fae there. They must've cost him a fortune.

ROSE. Certainly, we'll come along, eh, lassies? Any excuse for a party. Will there be free samples?

DES-NEIGES. I don't know. I suppose there might be. But I'll be makin up sandwiches.

ROSE. That's more nor ye get here. We'll be lucky tae get a glass ae water.

OLIVINE *tries to bite her daughter-in-law.*

THERESE. Mme. Dubuc, if you dinnae stop daein that I'm gaunnae lock ye in the lavvie an ye can stay there the rest ae the night.

Blackout.

Spotlight on DES-NEIGES.

DES-NEIGES. The first time I seen him I thought he was ugly. At least, I didnae think he was guid-lookin tae start wi. When I opened the door he took off his hat an said tae me, 'Would the lady of the house be interested in buying some brushes?' I shut the door in his face. I never allows a man intae ma hoose. Ye never know what might happen . . . The only one 'at gets in is the paper boy. He's still owre young tae get any funny ideas. Anyhows, a month later back he came wi his brushes. It was bucketin ootside so I let him stand in the lobby. Once he was in the hoose, I started tae get jittery, but I tellt masel he didnae look the dangerous type, even if he wasnae very bonny tae look at . . . But he ayeways looks that smart. No a hair oot ae place. Like a real gentleman. And he's ayeways that polite. Well, he selled me a couple ae brushes an then he showed me his catalogue. There was somethin 'at I wanted but he didnae have it wi him so he said I could order it. Ever since then, he's come back once a month. Sometimes I dinnae buy anythin. But he jist comes in an we blether for a wee while. He's an awful nice man . . . I think . . . I really think I'm in love wi him . . . I know it's daft . . . I only see him once a month . . . But it's that nice when we're thegither. I'm that happy when he comes. I've never felt like this afore. It's the first time it's happened tae me. For usual men've never paid me any notice. I've aye been . . . on the shelf, so tae speak. He tells me all aboot his trips, an all kinna stories an jokes. Sometimes his jokes are a wee bit near the bone, but they're that funny! I don't know why, but I've always liked jokes that are a wee bit dirty. It's good for ye, tae, for tae tell dirty jokes noo an again. Mind you, no all his jokes are dirty. Lots ae them are clean. An it's only jist recent he's started tellin me the dirty ones. Sometimes they're that dirty I blush red as a beetroot. The last time he tellt me one he took ma hand cause I blushed. Well, I vernear died. Ma insides went all funny when he put his big hand on mines. I need him sae much! I don't want him tae go away! Sometimes, jist noo an again, I dream aboot him. I dream . . . that we're married. I need him tae come back an see me. He's the first man 'at's ever paid me any notice. I don't want tae lose him! I dinnae want tae lose him! If he goes away, I'll be left on ma own again, and I need . . . somedy tae love . . . (*She lowers her eyes and murmurs*) I need a man.

The lights come back on. Enter LINDA, GINETTE *and* LISE.

GERMAINE. So ye've come back! No afore time, tae!

LINDA. I was at the cafe.

GERMAINE. I know damn fine ye were at the cafe. If ye keep hangin around there, ma lass, ye're gaunnae end up like your Auntie Pierrette . . . on the game.

LINDA. Leave off, mum! Your gettin worked up aboot nothin.

GERMAINE. I asked you tae stay in the hoose . . .

LINDA. Look, I jist went oot for fags an I bumped intae Lise and Ginette . . .

GERMAINE. That's nae excuse. You knew I was havin folk in. Ye shoulda come straight hame. You dae it on purpose, Linda. Ye dae it jist tae annoy me. Ye want tae make me lose ma temper in front ae ma friends. That's it, intit? Ye want tae make me swear in front ae ootsiders. Well, by Christ, you've succeeded! But dinnae you think I'm finished wi you yet, ma hen. I'll take care ae you later, Linda Lauzon, an you'll get what's comin tae ye.

ROSE. This isnae the place tae be gien her a bawlin oot, Germaine!

GABRIELLE. You! Keep your neb oot ae other folk's business.

LINDA. Help ma God! I'm jist two three minutes late. It's no the end ae the world.

LISETTE. It's our fault.

GERMAINE. Fine I know it's your faults. If I've tellt oor Linda once I've tellt her a thousand times no tae run around wi tramps. But do you think she pays a blind bit ae notice? She does everything tae contradict me. Sometimes I could strangulate her!

ROSE. Aw, come on, Germaine.

GABRIELLE. Rose, I've jist done tellin ye tae keep your nose oot ae this. It's their business. It's got nothin tae dae wi you.

ROSE. Stop nigglin me. You're gettin on ma tits. Why should Linda get bawled oot? She's done nothin wrong.

GABRIELLE. It's none ae oor business.

LINDA. You leave her alone, Auntie Gaby. She's only tryin tae stick up for us.

GABRIELLE. Don't you tell me what tae dae, young lady! You show some respect for your godmother.

GERMAINE. Ye see what she's like! She carries on this way all the time. I never brought her up tae act the goat like this.

ROSE. Aw aye, an how did ye bring your weans up?

GERMAINE. You! You're the one tae ask that question. Your weans . . .

LINDA. On ye go, Auntie Rose. You gie it tae her. Tell her straight. You the only 'at can dae it.

GERMAINE. What's come owre you all ae a sudden that you're sae thick wi your Auntie Rose? Have you forgotten what ye said when she phoned jist a wee while ago, eh? Come on, Linda, tell your Auntie Rose what ye said aboot her. Can ye no mind? Was it no . . .

LINDA. That was different.

ROSE. Why, what did she say?

GERMAINE. Well, she answered the phone when ye phoned earlier, mind? And she was owre ignorant tae say, 'One moment please', so I tellt her tae be more polite like . . .

LINDA. Och, shut up, mum! That's got nothin tae dae wi this.

ROSE. I want tae know what ye said, Linda.

LINDA. It wasnae anythin. I was getting at her. She was on ma back.

GERMAINE. She said, 'It's only ma Auntie Rose. I dinnae see why I should be polite tae her'.

ROSE. The cheeky wee bugger! Did you say that?

LINDA. I tellt ye, Auntie Rose. I was jist gettin at her.

ROSE. I'd never have thought that ae you, Linda. You've went doon in ma estimation. You've let me doon. You've really let me doon.

GERMAINE. Leave them tae fight it oot theirsels, Rose.

ROSE. Aye, I'll let them fight it oot. On ye go, Germaine. You gie it tae her, the wee gett! I'll tell you somethin, Linda. Your mother's right. If you dinnae watch your step, ye'll end up like your Auntie Pierrette. Count yoursel lucky I dinnae rattle your jaw here an noo.

GERMAINE. I'd like tae see ye try it! Naebody puts a hand on ma weans but me. If they need a leatherin, I'll gie it tae them. Naebody else has a right tae sae much as lay a finger on them.

THERESE. For-the-love-ae God, stop this argybargyin. I'm worn oot wi it.

DES-NEIGES. Me, tae. It's gien me palpitations.

THERESE. Ye're gaunnae wake up ma mother-in-law an she'll start her carry-on again.

GERMAINE. That's your look-oot, no mines! Ye shoulda left her at hame in the first place.

THERESE. Germaine Lauzon!

GABRIELLE. Well, she's quite right. Ye dinnae go oot tae parties wi a ninety-three year auld cripple.

LISETTE. Mme. Jodoin! And you're just done telling your sister to mind her own business.

GABRIELLE. Keep your big nose oot ae this, ya toffee-nosed gett! Jist you keep pastin thae stamps or I'll paste ye one in the mouth.

LISETTE *stands up.*

LISETTE. Gabrielle Jodoin!

OLIVINE, *who has been playing for a few minutes with a dish of water, lets it fall on the floor.*

THERESE. Watch oot what your daein, Mme. Dubuc.

GERMAINE. Aw Jesus wept! Ma tablecloth!

ROSE. She's soaked me, the auld bugger! I'm wringin wet.

THERESE. Nothin ae the kind. Ye were naewhere near!

ROSE. That's right, call me a liar tae ma face.

THERESE. It's true. Ye're nothin but a noted liar, Rose Ouimet.

GERMAINE. Watch, she's fallin oot her chair.

DES-NEIGES. Mary an Joseph, she's on the floor again!

THERESE. Somedy gie me a hand.

GABRIELLE. Pick her up yoursel.

DES-NEIGES. Here, I'll help ye, Mme. Dubuc.

THERESE. Thanks, Mlle. Verrette.

GERMAINE. Listen, Linda, you'd better stay oot ma road for the rest ae the night.

LINDA. Suits me. I cannae breathe in here. We'll go back tae the cafe.

GERMAINE. You dae that an you'll no set foot in this hoose again, d'ye hear?

LINDA. Aye, aye. I've heard it a thousand times.

LISETTE. Cut it oot, Linda . . .

THERESE. For-cryin-oot-loud, Mme. Dubuc, dinnae jist hang like that. Your daein it oot ae badness. Stiffen up, will ye.

MARIE-ANGE. I'll hold the chair.

THERESE. Thanks, hen.

ROSE. If it was up tae me, I'd take that stupid chair wi her in it and . . .

GABRIELLE. Dinnae you start again, Rose.

THERESE. Whew! What I have tae put up wi . . .

GABRIELLE. Hey, would ye get your full ae de Courval, still stickin her stamps . . . the stuck-up bitch. Ye'd think nothin had happened! I suppose this kinnae thing's beneath her.

Blackout.

Spotlight on LISETTE.

LISETTE. It's like living in a menagerie. My husband Léopold told me I shouldn't come, and he was right. These aren't our kind of people. They live in another world from us. When you've experienced life on a transatlantic liner and then compare it with this, well . . . It would make you weep . . . I can still see myself stretched out on my li-lo reading a Harold

Robbins . . . And that petty officer giving me the glad eye . . .
My husband says he was doing no such thing, but he couldn't
see all that I could see . . . Mmm . . . He was a fine figure of a
man . . . Maybe I should've egged him on a bit more . . . And
as for Europe! Everyone over there is so well brought up.
They're far more polite than here. You'd never meet a
Germaine Lauzon over there. Only people with class. In Paris
everyone speaks so refined. There they speak proper French . . .
No like here . . . I hate all of them. I'll never set foot in this
place again! Léopold was right. These people are inferior.
They're nothing but keelies. We shouldn't be mixing with
them. We shouldn't even waste breath talking about them . . .
They should be hidden away somewhere, out of sight. They
don't know what life is. We managed to pull ourselves up out
of this and we will make sure we never sink to their level again.
My God, I'm so ashamed of them.

The lights come back on.

LINDA. I've had enough. I'm leavin . . .

GERMAINE. I'm bloody sure'n ye're no! You've jist gaun owre
the score on purpose. I'm warnin you, Linda.

GERMAINE. 'I'm warnin you, Linda.' Is that all you can ever
say?

LISE. Dinnae be stupid, Linda.

GINETTE. Come on, let's stay.

LINDA. Naw, I'm gettin oot ae here. I've taen enough snash for
one night.

GERMAINE. Linda, I'm orderin you tae stay here!

VOICE OF A NEIGHBOUR. Are youse gaunnae stop that racket
up there! We cannae hear oorsels think!

ROSE *goes out on the balcony.*

ROSE. Hey, you! 'Way back intae your kennel!

NEIGHBOUR. I wasnae talkin tae you!

ROSE. Oh aye ye were. I was bawlin as loud as the rest ae them.

GABRIELLE. Rose, will you get in here!

DES-NEIGES. Dinnae pay any attention tae her.

NEIGHBOUR. I'm gaunnae send for the polis!

ROSE. Jist you go straight ahead. We could dae wi a few men up here.

GERMAINE. Rose Ouimet, you get back inside this hoose this instant! And you, tae, Linda . . .

LINDA. I'm for oot. Cheeriebye.

She leaves with GINETTE *and* LISE.

GERMAINE. She's went! Jist marched right oot, cool as ye like! Would ye credit it! She's tryin tae put me in ma grave, that wee besom. I'm gaunnae smash somethin! I'm gaunnae smash somethin!

ROSE. Get a grip ae yoursel, Germaine.

GERMAINE. Makin an arse oot ae me in front ae ootsiders! I'm black affronted!

She breaks down into tears.

That ma ain flesh'n'blood could dae that tae me . . . I'm that ashamed!

GABRIELLE. Come on noo, Germaine. It's no as bad as all that . . .

LINDA (*offstage*). Well, if it isnae Mademoiselle Sauvé! Hey-ya!

ANGELINE (*offstage*). Hullo, ma doll! How are ye?

ROSE. Germaine, they're here. Blow your nose an stop that greetin.

LINDA (*offstage*). Aw, no bad.

RHEAUNA (*offstage*). Where are ye off tae?

LINDA (*offstage*). I was gauntae go tae the cafe, but noo that you're here I think I'll stay.

Enter LINDA, GINETTE, LISE, RHEAUNA *and* ANGELINE.

ANGELINE. Hullo, evrubdy.

RHEAUNA. Hullo.

THE OTHERS. Hullo, hullo. How are yese? . . .

RHEAUNA. That's some climb up thae stairs, Mme. Lauzon. I'm fair peched.

GERMAINE. Well, jist sit yoursels doon an have a seat.

ROSE. Ye'll no have tae pech up the stairs the next time ye come. Ma sister'll see tae that. She's gaunnae get a lift put in wi her stamps.

The women laugh except for RHEAUNA *and* ANGELINE *who do not know how to take this comment.*

GERMAINE. Aw, very funny, Rose! Linda, away ben the hoose and get some more chairs . . .

LINDA. Where fae? There arenae nae more . . .

GERMAINE. Go an ask Mme. Bergeron if she'll lend us one or two.

LINDA. Come on youse pair . . .

GERMAINE (*in a low voice to* LINDA). Aw right, I'm holding my tongue the noo, but jist you look oot when the others leave.

LINDA. Look, I came back because Mlle. Sauvé and Mlle. Bibeau arrived, no cause I was feart ae you.

LINDA *goes out with* LISE *and* GINETTE.

DES-NEIGES. Here, have ma seat, Mlle. Bibeau . . .

THERESE. Aye, come an sit aside me for a wee while . . .

MARIE-ANGE. Sit doon here, Mlle. Bibeau . . .

ANGELINE & RHEAUNA. I see you're stickin stamps.

GERMAINE. Ye can say that again. A mullion ae them!

RHEAUNA. Good God, a mullion! How're yese gettin on?

ROSE. No bad, no bad . . . But ma tongue's paralysed . . .

RHEAUNA. Ye've licked all them wi your tongue?

GABRIELLE. Has she hell! She's jist actin the goat.

ROSE. She's as fast on the uptake as usual, that Bibeau.

ANGELINE. Can we gie ye a hand?

ROSE (*with a dirty laugh*). Dae ye no prefer lickin wi your tongue?

GABRIELLE. Your mind's filthy, Rose.

GERMAINE. And how did ye get on at the funeral parlour?

Blackout.

Spotlight on ANGELINE *and* RHEAUNA.

RHEAUNA. It came as a shock, I can tell ye.

ANGELINE. Ye didnae ken him that well though.

RHEAUNA. I kent his mother fine. So did you. Mind we went tae the school thegither, her an me? I watched that poor man growin up . . .

ANGELINE. Aye. It's a shame. Away jist like that. An us, we're still here, hanging on.

RHEAUNA. Ah, but no for long . . .

ANGELINE. Rhéauna, dinnae say things like that . . .

RHEAUNA. I ken what I'm talkin aboot. When ye've suffered as much as I have, ye can feel it when your time's nearly up.

ANGELINE. When it comes tae that, we've both had oor shares. I've suffered tae.

RHEAUNA. Aye, but I've suffered more nor you, Angéline. Seventeen operations. All I'm left wi is one lung, one kidney, one breast . . . you name it an I've had it oot. I'm tellin you, there's no much left ae me.

ANGELINE. And me wi ma arthritis 'at's aye gien me gyp. But Mme. . . . What's she cried? . . . Ken, the wife ae him 'at's dee'd? . . . She gied me the name ae a bottle tae get fae the chemist's. She said it would work wonders.

RHEAUNA. But ye ken fine ye've tried everythin. The doctors've all tellt ye there's nothin ye can dae aboot it. There's nae cure for arthritis.

ANGELINE. Doctors, doctors . . . I've had ma full o' doctors. All they're concerned aboot is makin money. They rook ye for all ye've got so's they can live in big hooses, drive fancy cars an fly away tae California for the winter. Dae you know, Rhéauna, that the doctor said he'd be up on his feet again in nae time, Monsieur . . . Monsieur . . . what was his name again? The one 'at's dee'd?

RHEAUNA. Monsieur Baril . . .

ANGELINE. Aye, that's it. I can never mind it. It's no as if it's difficult neither. Anyhow, the doctor tellt M. Baril that he had nothin tae worry aboot . . . An look what happened . . . Only forty year auld tae . . .

RHEAUNA. Forty year auld! That's owre young tae dee.

ANGELINE. He must have went doonhill in nae time at all.

RHEAUNA. She tellt me how it all happened. It would break your heart so it would . . .

ANGELINE. Is that a fact? I wasnae there when she tellt ye. How did it happen?

RHEAUNA. When he got hame fae's work on the Monday night, she thought he was a funny kinna colour. He was as white as a sheet, so she asked him if he was feelin awright. He said there was nothin wrong wi him, an they sat doon tae their tea . . . The kids were carryin on an argeyin at the table an Monsieur Baril lost the rag and leathered Rolande. That's his lassie. An, of course, it was then he took his turn . . . She says she didnae take her eyes off him for a second. She was watchin him like a hawk all the time but . . . She tellt me that it all was owre that quick that she didnae even have time tae move oot ae her seat. All of a sudden he said he was feeling funny and owre he cowped . . . His face landed right in his soup. An that was that!

ANGELINE. Holy Mother ae Mercy! Jist like that? That's no real. I'm tellin ye, Rhéauna, it's creepy. It makes ma flesh crawl. It gies me the heebie-jeebies.

RHEAUNA. There's a lesson in it jist the same though. We never ken when the good Lord's gaunnae come for us. As he said Himself, 'I'll come like a thief.'

ANGELINE. Oh, wheesht! It makes me feart, stories like that. I dinnae want tae die like yon. I want tae die in ma bed . . . Have time tae make a good confession.

RHEAUNA. Oh, please God dinnae let me die afore ma confession! Angéline, promise me ye'll get the priest in soon as I take no well. Promise me ye'll dae that.

ANGELINE. Och, ye ken I will. If ye've asked me once, ye've asked me a hundred times. Did I no get him for ye when ye had your last attack? He gien ye communion an everythin.

RHEAUNA. I'd be really feart tae die athoot receivin the last rites.

ANGELINE. Och, what've you got tae confess at your age, Rhéauna?

RHEAUNA. Age's got nothin tae dae wi it, Angéline. Sin disnae respect age.

ANGELINE. If ye ask me, Rhéauna, you'll go straight tae Heevin. You've got nothin tae worry aboot. Here, did ye notice that deed man's lassie? Monsieur what's his name? She looked like death warmed up.

RHEAUNA. I ken. Poor Rolande. She's gaun aboot tellin evrubdy she killed her father. It was cause ae her he lost his temper at the tea-table, ye see . . . Aw, I feel that sorry for her . . . And her mother. It's a cryin shame, so it is. It's a sore loss for them all . . . a sore loss.

ANGELINE. Aye, the heid ae the hoose, the father . . . you're tellin me. Mind you, it's no as bad as losin the mother, but still . . .

RHEAUNA. Right enough. Losin your mother's worser. Naebdy can take the place o' a mother.

ANGELINE. Did ye see how bonny he looked? . . . Like a young man. He was even smilin . . . Ye woulda thought he was jist sleepin. Still an all, I think he's better off where he is . . . It's true what they say, it's the ones 'at are left that deserve the sympathy. Him, he's safe noo . . . Oh, but I still cannae get owre hoo braw he looked. Ye'd hae actually thought he was still breathin.

RHEAUNA. Aye, but he wasnae.

ANGELINE. Mind you, I cannae for the life ae me see why they put him in thon suit.

RHEAUNA. What d'ye mean?

ANGELINE. Did ye no notice? He had on a blue suit. That's no the done thing. No for a deed man. A blue suit is far owre light. An if it has tae be blue, it should at least be navy blue . . . but no powder blue like thon. It's more decent for a deed man tae be dressed in a black suit.

RHEAUNA. Mebbe he didnae have one. They're no that well-off a family, ye ken.

ANGELINE. But for-the-love-ae-God, ye can hire a black suit! And did ye see Mme. Baril's sister? Dressed in green! In a chapel ae rest! An did ye notice how much she's aged? She looked years aulder than her sister . . .

RHEAUNA. But she is aulder.

ANGELINE. Dinnae haver, Rhéauna, she's a lot younger.

RHEAUNA. She's nothin ae the kind.

ANGELINE. I'm tellin ye, Rhéauna. Mme. Baril is thirty-seven comin on thirty-eight, and her sister . . .

RHEAUNA. She's well owre forty!

ANGELINE. Rhéauna, she isnae!

RHEAUNA. Well, I'd put her at forty-five.

ANGELINE. That's what I'm tryin tae tell ye. She's aged that much she looks more auld than she is . . . For look, ma guid-sister, Rose-Aimée, is thirty-six an the two ae them went tae the school thegither . . .

RHEAUNA. Well, whatever, I'm no surprised she's aged sae fast . . . What wi the life she leads . . .

ANGELINE. I'm no sure that all thae stories aboot her is true.

RHEAUNA. They must be! Mme. Baril tries tae hide it cause it's her sister . . . But the truth aye comes oot. It's like Mme. Lauzon an her sister, Pierrette. If there's one person I cannae stomach, it's that Pierrette Guerin. She's a right wee hure. Brought nothin but shame tae her family. I can tell you, Angéline, I wouldnae want tae see her soul. It must be as black as hell.

ANGELINE. Aw come on noo, Rhéauna, Pierrette isnae *all* bad.

Spotlight on GERMAINE.

GERMAINE. I've had nothin adae wi ma sister Pierrette for a long time noo. No after all she did tae us. An tae think that she was that well-behaved as a wean. She was as good as gold . . . butter wouldnae've melted in her mouth. An she was that bonny tae look at tae. But noo? Noo she's nothin but a wee hure. Me an ma sisters worshipped her. We spoilt her somethin rotten. I jist don't understand what went wrong. I jist don't understand. Ma father used tae call her his wee cooshie-doo. He was daft on her, his wee Pierrette. When he had her on his knee, ye could see hoo happy he was. An the rest ae us didnae even feel jealous . . .

Spotlight on ROSE.

ROSE. We used tae say tae oorsels, 'She's the baby ae the family so she's the favourite. That's jist the way ae it. The youngest aye gets the attention.' When she started the schuil, we dressed her up like a wee princess. I was already married by that time but I can mind on it as if it were jist yesterday. Oh, she was that bonny! A real Shirley Temple! An she learned that quick at the schuil. No like me. I never did a stroke at school . . . I was the class comic . . . That's all I've ever been good for. But her, the wee bugger, she was aye comin hame wi prizes. Top ae the class in French, in Arithmetic, in Religious Studies. Aye, Religious Studies! She was as religious an well-behaved as a nun, that wean. The Holy Sisters were daft on her, tae. If they could see her the day, though . . . My God, deep doon I feel a bit sorry for her. She must greet for help sometimes . . . And she must get hellish lonely . . .

Spotlight on GABRIELLE.

GABRIEL When she left the schuil, we asked her what she wanted tae be. She said she wanted tae be a teacher. She was all set tae start her trainin . . . but then she had tae go an meet that Johnny!

THE THREE SISTERS. That swine, Johnny! He's the work ae the devil! He's the one tae blame for her turnin oot the way she did. That bastardin Johnny! That bastardin Johnny!

RHEAUNA. What d'ye mean, no *all* bad! Ye've got tae sink gey low tae dae what she did. If you but kent what Mme. Longpré tellt me aboot her.

ANGELINE. Oh? How d'ye mean?

THERESE. Oh-ya!

The lights come back on. THERESE *skelps her mother-in-law on the head.*

GERMAINE. Thérèse, for once an for all make her behave hersel. Knock her senseless if ye've got tae, jist for Christ's sakes dae somethin.

THERESE. Aw aye, knock her senseless! Listen, I'm daein all I can tae keep her quiet. I'm no gaunnae kill her jist tae keep you happy.

ROSE. If she was mines, I'd throw her owre the balcony . . .

THERESE. You'd dae what? I didnae catch that, Rose Ouimet. What was it you said?

ROSE. I was talkin tae mysel.

THERESE. You're feart, eh?

ROSE. Me, feart?

THERESE. Aye, you! Feart!

MARIE-ANGE. Don't say there's gauntae be another rammy.

ANGELINE. How? Has there been a fight awready?

RHEAUNA. Who's been rammyin, then?

ANGELINE & RHEAUNA. We shoulda got here earlier.

THERESE. I'm no gaunnae sit here an take that. She's jist insulted ma mother-in-law! Ma man's mother!

LISETTE. Here they go again!

ROSE. She's senile! She should be put doon!

GERMAINE. Rose!

GABRIELLE. Ye should be doonright ashamed ae yoursel sayin somethin like that. Ye've got a heart ae stone.

THERESE. I'll never forgive you for what you jist said, Rose Ouimet. Never.

ROSE. For-the-love-ae-Christ, gie me patience!

ANGELINE. So who was fightin afore, eh?

ROSE. Aw you've got tae know everythin. The trouble wi you, Mademoiselle Sauvé, is your nose is aye botherin ye!

ANGELINE. Mme. Ouimet! There's nae need for that!

ROSE. Ye want us tae gie ye the scandal so's your big mouth can blab it all owre the place. Is that no it?

RHEAUNA. Mme. Ouimet, it's no often I lose ma temper but I'll no allow ye tae insult ma pal.

MARIE-ANGE. I'll jist snaffle some while naebody's lookin.

GABRIELLE (*who sees her doing it*). What's that you're daein, Mme. Brouillette?

ROSE. Okay-doke, I've said enough. I'll hold ma tongue.

MARIE-ANGE. Wheesht! Take thir an keep quiet!

LINDA, GINETTE *and* LISE *arrive with the chairs. A lot of movement and noise. All the women change places and take advantage of the distraction to steal more booklets and stamps.*

Dinnae be feart! Take some!

DES-NEIGES. Is this no gaun owre the score?

THERESE. Hide thir, Mme. Dubuc . . . Naw, Mme. Dubuc! I said hide them!

GERMAINE. See that fellie 'at runs the butcher's shop? He's a daylight robber . . .

The door opens suddenly. PIERRETTE *comes in.*

PIERRETTE. Hullo, everybody!

THE OTHERS. Pierrette!

LINDA. Ma Auntie Pierrette! This'll be rare!

ANGELINE. Oh my God, no Pierrette!

GERMAINE. Who tellt you tae come here? I tellt you afore I never wanted tae clap eyes on you again.

PIERRETTE. A wee bird tellt me that ma big sister, Germaine, had won a mullion stamps, so I decided tae come an see for masel. (*She notices* ANGELINE SAUVE.) Well, I'll be buggered! Angéline! What are you daein here?

Everyone stares at ANGELINE.

ACT TWO

The second act begins with PIERRETTE's *entrance again and a repeat of the last six lines of Act One, before continuing the action.*

The door opens suddenly. PIERRETTE *comes in.*

PIERRETTE. Hullo, everybody!

THE OTHERS. Pierrette!

LINDA. Ma Auntie Pierrette! This'll be rare!

ANGELINE. Oh my God, no Pierrette!

GERMAINE. Who tellt you tae come here? I tellt you afore I never wanted tae clap eyes on you again.

PIERRETTE. A wee bird tellt me that ma big sister, Germaine, had won a mullion stamps, so I decided tae come an see for masel. (*She notices* ANGELINE SAUVE.) Well, I'll be buggered! Angéline! What are you daein here?

Everyone stares at ANGELINE.

ANGELINE. Oh dear God! I've been found oot.

GERMAINE. How d'ye mean, Angéline?

GABRIELLE. What gies you the right tae think ye can talk tae Mlle. Sauvé like that?

ROSE. Ye've nae shame!

PIERRETTE. Why should I no talk tae her? Her an me are good pals, aren't we no, Géline?

ANGELINE. Oh! I think I'm gauntae faint.

ANGELINE *pretends to faint.*

RHEAUNA. Sweet Jesus, Angéline!

ROSE. She's deid!

RHEAUNA. Aw, naw . . .

GABRIELLE. She's nothin ae the kind. Rose, you're jist gaun too far again.

PIERRETTE. Anybody can see she's no fainted. She's jist play-actin.

PIERRETTE *goes over to* ANGELINE.

GERMAINE. Don't you lay a finger on her!

PIERRETTE. Leave me alone. She's ma pal.

RHEAUNA. What d'ye mean, your pal?

GERMAINE. You're no tryin tae tell us that Mademoiselle Sauvé is any friend ae yours!

PIERRETTE. Aw, but she is! She comes tae see's at the Club jist aboot every Friday night.

ALL THE WOMEN. Eh!

PIERRETTE. Ask her yoursel. Is that no the truth, Géline? Come on, stop actin the eejit an answer me. Angéline, we all know you're jist kiddin on. You tell them. Intit true you often come tae the Club?

ANGELINE *(after a silence)*. Aye, it's true.

RHEAUNA. Oh, Angéline! Angéline!

SOME WOMEN. This is hellish bad!

OTHER WOMEN. This is dia-bloody-bolical!

LINDA, GINETTE & LISE. This is magic!

Blackout.

RHEAUNA. Angéline! Angéline!

Spotlight on ANGELINE *and* RHEAUNA.

ANGELINE. Rhéauna, ye've got tae understand . . .

RHEAUNA. Dinnae come near me! Get away!

THE WOMEN. Who'd've thought it . . . A thing like that!

RHEAUNA. I'd never thought it ae you. You, in that Club. An every Friday night at that. It cannae be true.

ANGELINE. I dinnae dae anythin wrong, Rhéauna. I jist have a Coke.

THE WOMEN. In a Club!

GERMAINE. God alone knows what she gets up tae there.

ROSE. Mebbe she's on the game.

ANGELINE. But I'm tellin yese, I dae nothin wrong.

PIERRETTE. It's true, she does nothin wrong.

ROSE, GERMAINE & GABRIELLE. You shut up, ya Jezebel!

RHEAUNA. You're no ma pal nae more, Angéline. I don't know you.

ANGELINE. Listen tae me, Rhéauna, ye've got tae listen tae me! I can explain everything. If ye'll jist gie me a chance, then ye'll understand.

ROSE, GERMAINE & GABRIELLE. A Club! The quickest road tae the burnin fire!

ALL THE WOMEN (*except the young ones*). The road tae the burnin fire, the road tae the burnin fire. If ye go there, ye'll lose your soul. It's a sin tae drink, a sin tae dance! It's in thae Clubs oor menfolk fuddle their heids wi drink and lash oot their pays on hures an tramps.

ROSE, GERMAINE & GABRIELLE. Hures and tramps like you, Pierrette!

ALL THE WOMEN (*except the four young ones*). Dae you no think black burnin shame, Angéline Sauvé, tae've darkened the door ae thon den o' sin?

RHEAUNA. Angéline, a Club! It's worser than Hell itsel!

PIERRETTE (*laughing loudly*). If Hell's anythin like the Club I work in, I wouldnae say no tae bein condemned tae an eternity there!

ROSE, GERMAINE & GABRIELLE. Shut up, Pierrette. It's the devil's inside ye.

LINDA, GINETTE & LISE. The devil? Aw come off it! Grow up, will yese. The Clubs arenae as bad as yese make oot. They're nae worse nor anywhere else. They're jist for enjoyment. They're for enjoyin yoursels. That's all, they're for enjoyment.

THE WOMEN. Ach! Youse are owre young tae know! Owre young tae know! But yese'll find oot, ya young know-alls. Yese'll find oot an come greetin tae us. But it'll be owre late! Owre late! Jist you watch your steps in thae hellish holes. Yese'll no realise when yese is slippin, but when yese tries tae crawl back up, yese'll find oot it's owre late!

LISE. Too late! Too late! Oh my God, it's too late.

GERMAINE. The least you can dae is tae go tae confession, Angéline Sauvé!

ROSE. And tae think that I see you every Sunday at Mass . . . Mass wi a sin like thon on your conscience!

GABRIELLE. A mortal sin!

ROSE, GERMAINE & GABRIELLE. How many times dae ye need tae be tellt? . . . It's a mortal sin tae set foot inside a Club!

ANGELINE. Look, gie me a chance tae explain. Jist hear me oot.

THE WOMEN. Nut! Ye've nae excuse!

ANGELINE. Rhéauna, will you no listen tae me! We're auld pals. We've been friends for the past thirty-five year. I'm fond ae ye, but sometimes I feel like meetin other folk. Ye know what I'm like. I like tae have a bit ae fun noo an again. When I was young I kent nothin but the hoose an the chapel. There must be more tae life nor that. Ye can go tae Clubs wi'oot daein any harm. The Clubs arenae as bad as they're painted, ye know. I've been gaun tae them for the past four year an I've never done a thing I'm ashamed ae. The folk 'at works there are nae worse than you or me. I jist wanted tae get oot the bit an meet different folk, Rhéauna! I've never had any enjoyment oot ma life till the Club, Rhéauna!

RHEAUNA. There are better-like places tae enjoy yoursel. You'll pay for it when you're in burnin hell, Angéline. Promise me ye'll no go back there again.

ANGELINE. Look, Rhéauna, I cannae! I like for tae go there, dae ye no understand. I like it!

RHEAUNA. Ye've got tae promise me or I'll never speak tae ye again. It's up tae you. Ye've got tae make up your mind. It's either me or the Club. If you kent how much you've hurt me, ma bestest pal sneakin oot tae a Night Club ahint ma back. How d'ye think that looks, Angéline, eh? What d'ye think folk'll say when they see ye creepin intae a place like that, eh? Specially that joint where Pierrette works . . . It's a dive . . . The lowest ae the low. You've never tae go back, Angéline, d'ye hear me? If you dae, that's it, it's finished atween you an me. Finished! You should be doonright ashamed ae yoursel!

ANGELINE. Dinnae ask me no tae go back there, Rhéauna . . . Rhéauna, speak tae me!

RHEAUNA. I'm no sayin another word until you promise!

The lights return to normal. ANGELINE *sits in a corner,* PIERRETTE *joins her.*

ANGELINE. Why did you have tae come here the night for?

PIERRETTE. Let them yap. They like nothin better'n gettin worked up intae a tiz an blacknin folks' names. They know bloody fine you dae nothin wrong at the Club. Gie them five minutes an they'll have forgotten all aboot it.

ANGELINE. Aw aye, an ye think sae? Ye think Rhéauna'll change her mind? Ye think she'll forgie me jist like that? An Madame de Courval 'at's in charge ae recreation for the parish an is President ae the Altar Society at Oor Lady o' Perpetual Succour? Ye think she'll go on speakin tae me? An your sisters, 'at cannae be daein wi you cause ye work in a Club? I'm tellin ye, they're all finished wi me! Finished!

GERMAINE. Pierrette!

PIERRETTE. Listen, Germaine, Angéline feels bad enough athoot you an me gettin at each other's throats, right? I jist came here tae pay ye a visit an tae help ye stick your stamps, an that's all I'm gaunnae dae. An I've no got the pox, okay? Jist leave us alone. Us two'll stay in oor corner owre here. Ye neednae get your knickers in a twist. We'll stay oot ae your way. After the night, I'll no darken your door again, if that's the way ye want it . . . but I cannae leave Angéline in this state all herlane.

ANGELINE. Ye can go if ye want, Pierrette . . .

PIERRETTE. No, I want tae stay.

ANGELINE. Awright then, I'll go.

LISETTE. If only they'd both go!

ANGELINE *stands up.*

ANGELINE (*to* RHEAUNA). Are ye comin?

RHEAUNA *does not answer.*

Okay, I'll leave the door off the snib.

She goes towards the door. Blackout. Spotlight on ANGELINE.

It's easy tae criticise other folk. It's easy tae criticise them. But you've got tae look at it fae both sides. The folk I meet in that Club are ma best pals. Naebody's ever been sae nice tae me afore . . . No even Rhéauna. Wi thae folk I enjoys masel. I can laugh an joke wi them. I was brought up by nuns both in an oot the school. They did their bests tae learn me, poor souls, but they'd never lived. Dae you know, I was fifty-five year ae age afore I learned how tae enjoy masel. An that was only by luck, thanks tae Pierrette takin me tae her Club one night. Oh, I didnae want tae go. She had to drag me there. But, the minute I stepped owre that door, I kent what it was tae go through life athoot any enjoyment. Oh, I appreciate Clubs arenae everybody's cup ae tea, but me, I think they're great. 'Course, it's no the whole truth I only have a Coke when I goes there. Noo an again I haves a drink. No much, mind, but it fair cheers me up. It's no as if I dae any harm tae anybody. I jist buys masel two hours ae enjoyment a week. But this was bound tae happen sooner or later. I kent it. Dear God, what'm I gauntae dae. (*Pause.*) God Almighty! Everybody deserves tae get a wee bit enjoyment oot their lives! (*Pause.*) I aye tellt masel that if I got caught, I'd stop gaun tae the Club . . . But I'm no sure that I'll can stop . . . An Rhéauna wouldnae put up wi that. (*Pause.*) All an all, if it comes tae the bit, I suppose Rhéauna means more tae me nor Pierrette does. (*Long sigh.*) It looks like ma fun's finished . . .

She goes off.

Spotlight on YVETTE.

YVETTE. Ma guid-sister, Fleur-Ange, had her birthday party last week. It was a rare party. There was a big gang ae us there. Tae start wi, there was her an her family. Oscar David, that's her man, Fleur-Ange David, that's hersel, an their seven weans: Raymonde, Claude, Lisette, Fernand, Réal, Micheline, and Yves. Her man's folks, Aurèle David and his wife, Ozéla David were there tae. Then there was ma guid-sister's mother, Blanche Tremblay. Her father wasnae there, for he's deid. Then there was the rest ae us: Antonio Fournier, an his wife Rita, Germaine Gervais was there, tae, an Wilfred Gervais, Armand Gervais, George-Albert Gervais, Louis Thibault, Rose Campeau, Daniel Lemoyne an his wife, Rose-Aimée, Roger Joly, Hormidas Guay, Simonne Laflamme, Napoléon Gauvin, Anne-

Marie Turgeon, Conrad Joannette, Léa Liasse, Jeannette
Landreville, Nina Laplante, Robertine Portelance, Gilberte
Morrissette, Laura Cadieux, Rodolphe Quintal, Willie
Sanregret, Lilianne Beaupré, Virginie Latour, Alexandre
Thibodeau, Ovila Gariépy, Roméo Bacon an his wife, Juliette,
Mimi Bleau, Pit Cadieux, Ludger Champagne, Rosaire
Rouleau, Roger Chabot, Antonio Simard, Alexandrine Smith,
Philémon Langlois, Eliane Meunier, Marcel Morel, Grégoire
Cinq-Mars, Théodore Fortier, Hermine Héroux an us, me an
ma man, Euclide. That was jist aboot them all, I think . . .

The lights come back on.

GERMAINE. Awright noo, let's get back tae work again, eh?

ROSE. Aye, get your fingers oot an your tongues in!

DES-NEIGES. We're no daein that bad, are we? Look at the pile
I've done awready . . .

MARIE-ANGE. No tae mention the ones you've thieved . . .

LISETTE. Would you care to pass me over some more stamps,
Mme. Lauzon?

GERMAINE. Oh, aye . . . most certainly . . . Here's a whole pile.

RHEAUNA. Angéline! Angéline! It cannae be true!

LINDA (*to* PIERRETTE). Hullo Auntie Pierrette.

PIERRETTE. Hi-ya, doll. How're ye doin?

LINDA. Aw, no sae good. Ma mum an me's aye fightin. I'm sick
fed up ae it. She's aye greetin an girnin aboot nothin . . . ye
know what she's like. I wish I could jist clear oot ae here.

GERMAINE. It'll no be long afore the retreats'll be startin, eh
no?

ROSE. Aye. They were jist sayin that at Mass last Sunday there.

MARIE-ANGE. I hope it'll no be the same priest as last year 'at
comes.

GERMAINE. I hope not! I didnae take tae him neither. He'd put
ye tae sleep, yon yin.

PIERRETTE. Well, there's nothin holdin ye back fae leavin. Ye
could ayeways come an stay wi me . . .

LINDA. Are you kiddin? They'd turn their backs on me for good!

LISETTE. No, it's not the same one coming this year.

DES-NEIGES. Naw? Who is it then?

LISETTE. It's an Abbé Rochon. He's supposed to be wonderful. Abbé Gagné was just telling me the other day that he was one of his best friends . . .

ROSE (*to* GABRIELLE). There she goes again aboot her Abbé Gagné. We'll be hearin aboot him all night noo, nothin surer! Anybody'd think she fancied him. It's Abbé Gagné this, Abbé Gagné that . . . As far as I'm concerned, he's a right pain in the arse. I don't like him one bit.

GABRIELLE. Me neither. He's owre new-fangled in his ideas for me. It's one thing tae take an interest in your parishioners but it's another tae stick your nose intae parish business. He shouldnae forget that he's a priest. A man of higher things!

LISETTE. Oh, but the man is a saint . . . You should get to know him, Mme. Dubuc. I'm sure you'd take to him . . . When he speaks, you'd think it was the Lord God himself talking to you.

THERESE. Ye shouldn't exaggerate.

LISETTE. But it's the truth. Even the wee ones, the children, worship him . . . oh, that reminds me, the children of the parish are putting on a concert next month. I hope you'll all can come along. It should be a wonderful evening. They've already been practising for weeks . . .

DES-NEIGES. What are they gaunnae have?

LISETTE. Oh, lots of interesting things. They're going to perform all kinds of acts. Mme. Gladu's wee boy is going to sing . . .

ROSE. No again! I've had ma full ae that wee gett. He gies me the dry boke. I'm tellin ye, ever since he was on the TV his mother's walked around wi her nose in the air. Thinks she's a bigshot!

LISETTE. But little Raymond has a beautiful voice.

ROSE. Is that so? Well, if ye ask me he looks like a jessie, wi his mouth all screwed up like a duck's arse.

GABRIELLE. Rose!

LISETTE. Diane Aubin is going to give a demonstration of swimming in water . . . The concert is going to take place at the public baths . . . It's going to be beautiful . . .

ROSE. Will there be a raffle?

LISETTE. Oh, of course. And the last event of the evening will be a grand bingo.

THE OTHER WOMEN (*except the four young women*). A bingo!

OLIVINE. Bingo!

Blackout.

When the lights come back on, the nine women are standing at the edge of the stage.

LISETTE. An Ode to Bingo!

While ROSE, GERMAINE, GABRIELLE, THERESE *and* MARIE-ANGE *recite the Ode to Bingo, the four other women call out bingo numbers in counterpoint and very rhythmically.*

ROSE. Eyes down for a full house.

ROSE, GERMAINE, GABRIELLE, THERESE & MARIE-ANGE. For me, nothin beats a game ae bingo. There's one in oor parish every month. Two days afore, I start tae get on edge. I get that nervous an jittery. I cannae get it oot ma mind. When the big day comes I'm that excited I'm no able tae dae a hand's turn aboot the hoose. The minute the tea's past, I put ma glad-rags on an I'm oot the hoose in a shot. No even an atom bomb'd stop me. I'm daft on the bingo! I'm bingo-daft. There's nothin I like more than bingo! When we get there, it's coats off an a mad dive for a seat. Sometimes the livin-room's cleared for us, an sometimes the kitchen. It's even been known for us tae use the bedroom. We sit doon at the tables, hand round the cards, set up the balls, an away we go . . .

The women who are calling the numbers continue alone for a few seconds.

I get that excited I vernear hae a fit. I get all flustered. I come oot in a cold sweat. I mix up all the numbers. I put ma cross in the wrong boxes. I make the caller repeat the numbers for me. Oh, what a state I get intae! I'm daft on bingo! The game's aboot finished. Ma hoose is aboot up. I need jist a fourteen! All I want's a fourteen! Gie me a fourteen! A fourteen! I keek at the others . . . they're as close tae oot as me, the buggers. What'm I gaunnae dae? I've got tae win! I've got tae win! I've got tae win!

LISETTE. Fourteen!

THE FIVE WOMEN. House! House! I've won. I knew it! I knew I couldnae lose! I've won. What's the prize?

LISETTE. Last month was the month for standard lamps. But this month, wait for it, it's wally dogs!

THE NINE WOMEN. I'm daft on the bingo! I'm bingo-daft! There's nothin I like more than bingo! It's a shame they havnae bingo more often! The more bingo the better. Hip, hip, for the standard lamps! Hip, hip, for the wally dogs. Hip, hip, hooray for the bingo! Hip, hip, hooray for the bingo!

ROSE. Ma tongue's hangin oot wi thirst.

GERMAINE. Oh-tae-Christ, I forgot all aboot the drink. Linda, get the Cokes oot.

OLIVINE. Coke . . . Coke . . . aye, aye . . . Coke . . .

THERESE. Have patience, Mme. Dubuc. You'll get some Coke along wi everybody else. But jist you mind an drink it right, eh? Nae spillin it like ye did the last time.

ROSE. She's drivin me up the wall wi that mother-in-law ae hers. I'm no jokin.

GABRIELLE. Quit it Rose. There's been enough argybargyin the night as it is athoot you startin it again.

GERMAINE. Aye. Jist you keep quiet an stick thae stamps. Ye've scarce filled one book!

Spotlight on the fridge. The scene which follows takes place in front of the fridge door.

LISE (*to* LINDA). I've got tae talk tae ye, Linda.

LINDA. Aye, I know. Ye tellt me at the cafe . . . But this isnae the time, is it?

LISE. It'll no take long. I've got tae tell somebody. I cannae keep it tae masel much longer. I'm too worked up. You're ma best pal, Linda . . . I want you tae be the first tae know. Linda, I'm gaunnae have a wean.

LINDA. You're what? Naw, ye cannae be. Are ye sure?

LISE. Aye, I'm sure. The doctor tellt me.

LINDA. What're ye gaunnae dae?

LISE. I don't know. I'm that depressed, Linda. I havnae said anything tae ma ma an da yet. I'm feart what ma father'll dae. He'll murder me, so he will. An that's no kiddin. When the doctor tellt me I felt like jumpin oot the window there an then.

PIERRETTE. Listen, Lise . . .

LINDA. Did you hear?

PIERRETTE. Aye, I can appreciate how your feelin, hen, but . . . I might be able tae help ye . . .

LISE. Oh aye? How?

PIERRETTE. Well, I know a doctor . . .

LINDA. Auntie, you're no suggestin that!

PIERRETTE. Och, away! It's no dangerous . . . He does it two three times a week, this doctor.

LISE. I must admit I've awready thought aboot it . . . But I didnae know naebody tae approach . . . An I was feart tae try it masel.

PIERRETTE. Dinnae you ever try that! It's owre dangerous! But wi this doctor ae mines . . . If ye like, I can arrange it for ye. A week fae noo an ye'll be as right as rain.

LINDA. Lise, ye widnae want tae dae that, would ye? It's criminal!

LISE. What else would ye have me dae? What choice have I got? It's the only way oot. I don't want the wean. Look what happened tae Manon Belair. She was in the same position an noo her life's wasted cause she's lumbered wi that kid.

LINDA. But what aboot the father? Would he no marry ye?

LISE. Ye know fine he dropped us. He beat it soon's he found oot. Naebody seems tae know where he's went. When I think ae the promises he made us. How happy we were gaunnae be thegither, an how he was makin money hand-owre-fist. Eejit that I am, I taen it all in. It was presents here, presents there . . . there was nae end tae them. Aw, it was nice enough at the time . . . in fact, it was really nice . . . But bugger it, then this had tae happen. I jist knew it would. I've never been gien a break. Never. Why is it me ayeways lands heidfirst in the shite when all I want tae dae is climb oot ae it? I'm bloody well sick ae workin behind the counter in that shop. I want tae dae

somethin wi ma life. D'ye understand? I want tae get
somewhere. I want a car, a nice flat, some nice claes. Christ
knows, aboot all I've got tae put on ma back are shop overalls.
I've aye been hard up . . . aye had tae scrimp'n scrape . . . But
I'm damn sure I'm no gaunnae go on like this. I don't want tae
be a naebody any more. I've had enough ae bein poor. I'm
gaunnae make sure things gets better. I was mebbe born at the
bottom ae the pile but I'm gaunnae climb tae the top. I came
intae this world bi the back door but by Christ I'm gaunnae go
oot bi the front. An ye can take it fae me that nothin's gaunnae
get in ma way. Nothin. You wait, Linda. Jist you wait. You'll see
I'm no kiddin. In two three years you'll see that Lise Paquette's
become a somebody. Jist you watch, she'll be rollin in it then.

LINDA. You're no gaun the right way aboot it.

LISE. But that's what I'm tryin tae tell ye. I've made a mistake an
I want tae put it right. After that I'm gaunnae make a new start.
You understand what I'm saying, Pierrette, don't ye?

PIERRETTE. Aye, I dae, hen. I understand what it is tae want tae
better yoursel. When I was your age I left hame because I
wanted tae make big money. But I didnae go aboot it by
workin in some two-bit shop. Nae danger! I went straight intae
the Club, for that's where the money was. An it'll no be long
noo till I'm rollin in it. Johnny himsel's promised me . . .

ROSE, GERMAINE & GABRIELLE. That swine Johnny! That
swine Johnny!

GINETTE. What are youse up tae owre here, eh?

LISE. No nothin. (*To* PIERRETTE.) We'll talk aboot it later on . . .

GINETTE. Aboot what?

LISE. It'll no matter. It's nothin.

GINETTE. Can ye no tell me?

LISE. You'd clype, so jist drop it, eh?

PIERRETTE. Come on, hen, you an me can talk it owre across
here . . .

GERMAINE. What's happenin tae thae drinks?

LINDA. They're comin, they're comin . . .

The lights come back on..

GABRIELLE. Aw, Rose, see that blue suit ae yours? How much did ye pay for it?

ROSE. What one?

GABRIELLE. Ye know, the one wi the white lace round the collar.

ROSE. Oh, that yin . . . I got it for $9.98.

GABRIELLE. That's what I thought. Would ye believe I seen the same one the day in Reitmans for $14.98 . . .

ROSE. Get away! I tellt ye I'd picked it up cheap, eh?

GABRIELLE. You're a dab hand at findin bargains, right enough.

LISETTE. My daughter, Micheline, has just started a new job. She's working on those F.B.I. machines.

MARIE-ANGE. Is that a fact! I've heard tell they go for your nerves, thae machines. The lassies 'at work on them have tae change jobs every six month. Ma guid-sister Simonne's daughter had a nervous breakdown owre the heid ae one. Simonne was jist on the phone the day tellin me aboot it . . .

ROSE. Oh, buggeration, that minds me. Linda, you're wanted on the phone.

LINDA *rushes to the telephone.*

LINDA. Hullo, Robert? How long've ye been waitin?

GINETTE. Come on, tell me.

LISE. Naw. Beat it, will ye? Stop hangin aboot me. I want tae talk tae Pierrette for a wee while. Goan, hop it, buggerlugs.

GINETTE. Awright, I can take a hint. It's no that, though, when you've got naebody tae talk tae, intit no? But as soon as somebody else comes along . . .

LINDA. Look Robert, for the fifth time, it's no ma fault! I'm tellin ye, I jist this minute was tellt ye were on the phone!

THERESE. Here, Mme. Dubuc, hide thir!

ROSE (*to GINETTE who is handing out the drinks*). How're things at hame, Ginette?

GINETTE. Aw, jist the same as ever . . . They fight like cat'n dog all day . . . Same as usual. Ma mother still hits the bottle . . . an ma father still goes off the deep-end at her . . . They'll be fightin wi each other till their dyin days . . .

ROSE. Ya poor thing ye . . . An your sister?

GINETTE. Suzanne? Aw, she's still the brainy one ae the family. They think the sun shines oot ae her arse. She cannae dae naething wrong, her. They cannae see past her. 'How can ye no be more like her, Ginette, an use your heid. Ye should learn fae her. She's makin somethin ae her life.' Me, I'm a nothin as far as they're concerned. But I've aye knew they've thought more ae her nor me. But noo that she's a schuil-teacher, it's got beyond a joke.

ROSE. Aw, come on, Ginette. D'ye no think your exaggeratin it a wee bit?

GINETTE. Naw, I know what'm sayin . . . Ma mother's never had any time for me. It's ayeways been 'Suzanne's the bonniest. Suzanne's the most refined'. I've heard it day in day oot till I'm sick ae hearin it! An tae cap it all, noo even Lise disnae like me anymore.

LINDA (*on the phone*). Away you tae hell! Go on, bugger off! If you dinnae want tae listen, why should I bother tae explain? What more dae ye want me tae sae? Ye can phone back when you're in a better mood!

She hangs up.

For-cryin-oot-loud, Auntie Rose, ye coulda tellt me I was wanted on the phone! He bawled me oot, an noo he's taken the huff at me!

ROSE. Would ye listen tae her! Who does she thing she's talkin tae? She's doo-lally, that yin!

Spotlight on PIERRETTE.

PIERRETTE. When I left hame I was that in love ma heid was back tae front. I couldnae see straight. I'd eyes for naebody but Johnny. Naebody else counted. That bastard made me squander ten years ae ma life. Here I am, only thirty year ae age, an I feels like sixty. The things that chancer got me tae dae for him. I was aye taen in by his patter, eejit that I am. Ten year I knocked ma guts oot in his Club for him. I was smashin lookin then. I drew his customers in an that kept him sweet as long as it lasted. But as for that bastard noo, I've had ma full. I'm sick-scunnert . . . Deid-done cawin ma pan oot, an for what? All I feel fit for is jumpin off a bridge. It's jist the drink that keeps me gaun. I've been on the bottle solid since last

Friday past. And that poor Lise thinks she's all washed up just cause she's pregnant! Christ Almighty, she's young yet! I'm gaunnae gie her ma doctor's name'n address . . . He'll see her right. She'll can make a new start. No me, though. If ye've been at it for ten year, ye're owre the hill. A has-been. But how could I even begin tae explain that tae ma sisters? They'd never understand. No in a month ae Sundays. I don't know what I'm gaunnae dae noo. What'm I tae dae?

LISE (*at the other end of the kitchen*). I don't know what I'm gaunnae dae noo. What am I tae dae? An abortion's a serious matter. Specially if ye try tae dae it yoursel. I've heard enough stories tae know that. I'd be safer tae go an see this doctor ae Pierrette's. Aw, why dae thir things aye happen tae me? Pierrette's lucky. Workin in that Club for ten year. Makin loads ae money. An she's in love, tae! I wouldnae say no tae bein in her shoes. Even if her family havnae nae time for her, at least she's happy being on her ain.

PIERRETTE. He chucked me oot, jist like that! 'It's all finished,' he said. 'You're nae more use tae me. You're too auld noo an past your best. So ye can pack your bags an beat it. You're no wanted.' The heartless gett! He didnae leave me wi a cent! Not a cent! The bastard! After all that I did for him owre the past ten year! Ten year for sweet bugger-all! If that wouldnae make ye want tae dae away wi yoursel, what would? What'm I tae dae? Eh, jist what? Stand at the back ae a counter all day like Lise? Become a shop-assistant? No thank you! Nae danger! That's awright for young bit lassies an auld women, but no for me. What'm I tae dae? I've jist nae idea. I've got tae put a face on it here. I cannae tell the truth tae Linda and Lise or I'm all washed up. (*Silence.*) Aye, well . . . there's nothin left but the drink noo . . . Guid job I like the stuff . . .

LISE (*repeating several times throughout* PIERRETTE's *last monologue*). Oh, Sweet Jesus, I'm feart! (*She goes up to* PIERRETTE *and throws herself into her arms.*) Are you sure this is gaunnae work, Pierrette? I'm feart, so I am!

PIERRETTE (*laughing*). Aye, aye. Everthing'll be jist fine, hen. You'll see. Everything'll be okay . . .

The lights return to normal.

MARIE-ANGE (*to* DES-NEIGES). Dae you know, it's no even safe tae go tae the pictures. Jist the other day I went tae see Yves Montand in somethin . . . I cannae mind the name ae it. Ma man wasnae interested so he stayed at hame. Well, here, would ye credit, right in the middle ae the picture, this auld bugger comes an sits asides me, an afore I know what's gaun on, he starts playin wi ma knee, anglin for a feel. I was as embarrassed as get oot, as ye can well imagine, but I kept ma heid. I stood up an belted him one in his ugly puss wi ma handbag.

DES-NEIGES. Guid for you, Mme. Brouillette! I ayeways carries a hatpin when I go tae the pictures. Ye can never tell what might happen. The first one 'at tries any funny stuff wi me . . . Mind you, I've never had tae use it yet.

ROSE. This Coke is braw an warm, Germaine.

GERMAINE. When are you gaunnae stop criticisin, eh? Jist when, tell me?

LISE. Linda, have you got a pencil an paper?

LINDA. Look, Lise, I'm tellin ye, dinnae dae it!

LISE. I know what I'm daein. I've made ma mind up an nothin'll make me change it.

RHEAUNA (*to* THERESE). I'm no a thief!

THERESE. Aw, come on, Mlle. Bibeau, it's no thievin. It's no as if she payed anything for thir stamps. An she's got a mullion after all. A mullion!

RHEAUNA. That's nothin tae dae wi it! She invited us here tae help her stick her stamps for her an we've nae right tae turn round an start thievin them.

GERMAINE (*to* ROSE). What are they two up tae? I dinnae like all this whisperin . . .

She approaches RHEAUNA *and* THERESE.

THERESE (*seeing her coming*). Oh . . . Aye . . . Ye add two cups ae water an then stir it.

RHEAUNA. Eh? Ye what? (*Noticing* GERMAINE.) Oh! Aye! she was jist gien me a recipe.

GERMAINE. A recipe? For what?

RHEAUNA. Doughnuts!

THERESE. A chocolate puddin!

GERMAINE. Well, which is it tae be? Doughnuts or chocolate puddin?

She goes back to ROSE.

Listen Rose, there's some funny business gaun on here the night.

ROSE (*who has just hidden a few booklets in her handbag*). Dinnae be daft . . . You're imaginin things . . .

GERMAINE. An I think Linda's spendin too much time wi oor Pierrette tae. Linda, come owre here!

LINDA. Hang on a minute, Mum . . .

GERMAINE. I tellt you tae come here! That means now! No the morra!

LINDA. Awright, awright! Keep your heid on . . . Aye, what is it?

GABRIELLE. Keep us company for a wee while . . . You've been wi your auntie for long enough . . .

LINDA. So? What's that tae you?

GERMAINE. What's gaun on atween her an your pal, Lise, owre there?

LINDA. Oh . . . nothin . . .

GERMAINE. You answer me straight when you're spoken tae!

ROSE. Lise wrote somethin doon a wee while ago.

LINDA. It was jist an address.

GERMAINE. Dinnae tell me she's taen Pierrette's address! Look you, if I ever find oot you've been at her place, you'll hear aboot it, d'ye understand?

LINDA. Will you leave me alone! I'm auld enough tae know what I'm daein!

She goes back towards PIERRETTE.

ROSE. It's mebbe none ae ma business, Germaine, but . . .

GERMAINE. But what? What's wrong noo?

ROSE. Your Linda's startin tae go owre the score . . .

GERMAINE. Dae I no know it! But dinnae you worry, Rose. I can handle her. She's gaunnae get put in her place pronto. An as for that Pierrette, this is the last time she'll set foot in this hoose. After the night, that's her oot for good.

MARIE-ANGE. Have ye had a look at Mme. Bergeron's daughter jist recent? Would ye no say she'd kinna puttin on the beef, so tae speak?

LISETTE. Yes, I've noticed that . . .

THERESE (*insinuatingly*). It's funny that, intit? Specially the way the fat's all gatherin round her belly.

ROSE. Well, ye know what they say . . . what goes up must come doon!

MARIE-ANGE. She tries tae hide it tae. But it's really startin tae stick oot.

THERESE. You're no kiddin! I wonder who did it tae her.

LISETTE. It'll most likely have been her step-father . . .

GERMAINE. That wouldnae surprise me one little bit. He's had his eye on her ever since he married her mother.

THERESE. It would turn your stomach what goes on in thon hoose. Poor Monique. She's jist a young lassie . . .

ROSE. Mebbe so, but she knows the score, that same yin. Jist look at the way she dresses. Last summer, by Christ, I was embarrassed jist lookin at her! An ye know me . . . I'm no easily shocked. D'ye no mind thae red shorts she was wearin all the time? Thae really tight ones? Well, I've said it afore an I'll say it again, that Monique Bergeron is gaunnae come tae a bad end. She's got badness in her, that lassie, pure badness. She's a redheid, of course, an ye know what they say aboot women wi red hair . . . Naw, yese can say what yese like, thae young lassies 'at gets up the stick afore they're married deserves all they get. I've nae sympathy for them.

LISE *makes a move to get up.*

PIERRETTE. Jist relax, hen!

ROSE. If ye ask me, they bring it on theirsels. I'm no talkin aboot the ones 'ats gets raped, mind. That's somethin allthegither different. But an ordinary lassie 'at gets hersel up the stick, naw, naw . . . I've got nae sympathy for her. It's her tough luck.

She's made her bed, an she can lie in it. I can tell you, if ma lassie Carmen ever came hame wi one up her, she'd go heid first oot the window in double-quick time! There's nae danger ae her gettin in that way, though. She'd never dae somethin dirty like that . . . She's as pure as the driven snow, that lassie. Naw, as far as I'm concerned all thae unmarried mothers are the same. They're a shower ae filthy hures! It's them that does the chasin after the men. Ye know what ma man calls them? Shag-bags!

LISE. If she disnae shut it, I'll kill her!

GINETTE. Why? If ye ask me, she's right.

LISE. You piss off afore I belt ye one!

PIERRETTE. That's a bit hard, is it no, Rose?

ROSE. Oh, aye, we all know you're the expert on thae kinnae things. Nothin'll surprise you . . . you've saw it all afore. It's mebbe normal tae you, but it's no tae us. There's only one way tae stop that sort ae thing happenin . . .

PIERRETTE (*laughing*). I know a lot ae ways. Have ye never heard tell ae the pill, for instance?

ROSE. Ach, it's nae use talkin tae you! You know damn fine that's no what I meant! I'm a good Catholic, an I'm against all this free love! Ya hure that ye are, ye can jist leave us alone an go back tae them ye belong with!

LISETTE. Just the same, Mme. Ouimet, I think you're maybe overdoing it. Sometimes it happens that girls who find themselves in the family way aren't themselves entirely to blame.

ROSE. You believe everythin they fill your heid with in thae stupid French fillums!

LISETTE. What have you got against French films, then?

ROSE. Nothin. I like American ones better, that's all. Thae French fillums are too realistic. They're nothin like real life. They exaggerate everythin. Ye shouldnae be taken in by them. They aye try tae make ye feel sorry for the lassie gets hersel pregnant. It's never anybody's fault as far as they're concerned. Jist ask yoursel, dae you think real life's like that? I'm damn sure I dinnae! A fillum's a fillum an life is life!

LISE. Jesus Christ, I'll murder that stupid bitch! The ignorant pig! She's the last one should go aboot judgin everybody. Her Carmen? Well, I know a lot aboot her Carmen awright an ye can take it fae me, she's had more cocks than hot dinners! She should redd up her ain midden afore she shites on everybody else's!

Spotlight on ROSE.

ROSE. Life is life, an nae bloody Frenchman ever made a fillum aboot that, or will! The man could show life the way it is, has yet tae be born. Aw aye, it's easy-peasy for any actress tae turn it on an make ye feel sorry for her in a fillum. Easy-bloody-peasy! But when she's finished work at night, she can go hame tae her big fancy mansion an climb intae her big fancy bed 'at's twice the bloody size ae ma bedroom! As for the rest ae us, when we get up in the mornin . . . (*Silence.*) When I wake up in the mornin, he's aye lyin there starin at me . . . Waitin. Every mornin that the Good Lord sends, I open ma eyes an there he is, waitin! Every night I get intae ma bed an there he is, waitin! He's aye there, aye after me, aye hangin owre me like a vulture. Bastardin sex! It's never like that in the fillums, though, is it? Oh no, that's the kinnae thing they never show. Who the hell's interested in a woman 'at's got tae see oot a life-sentence wi some filthy gett cause she said 'Aye' tae him once? Naw, that wouldnae be interestin enough for fillums. Christ knows, nae film was ever as sad as this. Nae film lasts a lifetime like this. (*Silence.*) I've often said it. Often. I should never have married. Never. I shoulda screamed it at the top ae ma voice: 'Never! Never!'. I'da been better off an auld spinster instead ae this. At least I'd a got some peace tae masel . . . been left alone. I didnae have a clue what I'd let masel in for. Young eejit that I was, all I could think aboot was 'the Holy State of Matrimony'! You've got tae be stupid bringin your weans up like that, knowin nothin. You've got tae be hellish stupid! But I'll tell you one thing, ma Carmen'll no get catched oot like me. I've been drummin it intae her for years what men are really like. She'll no end up like me, forty-four year ae age, wi a two-year-auld wean still on ma arm, an wi an ignorant swine ae a man whose heid's full ae nothin more than makin sure he gets his end away two an more times a day, three hunner an sixty-five day ae the year! When ye get tae be ma age an ye realise your life's been a nothin, an nothin it'll stay till ye die, it makes ye want tae pack the whole lot in an start all owre again. But a woman

cannae dae that . . . Fae start tae finish she's put under the
thumb, an there she's got tae stay right till the bitter end!

The lights come back on.

GABRIELLE. Well say what ye will, for masel I like French
pictures, specially the sad ones. They're smashin. They aye
make me greet. An ye've got tae admit thae Frenchmen're a lot
better-lookin than Canadians. They're real men, they are!

GERMAINE. Aw, hold on noo! I cannae let ye away wi that . . .

MARIE-ANGE. All thae Frenchmen are toattie. The wee nyaffs
dinnae come up tae ma shoulders even. An they act like jessies!
Pure jessies!

GABRIELLE. I beg your pardon. Some of them are real men! An
I don't mean like our useless menfolk!

GERMAINE. Ye can say that again! Compared tae oor men
anythin'd look guid! They're jist teuchters . . . they've nae style,
nae notion ae manners . . . Mind you, oor menfolk might be
coarse, but oor actors are just as guid an every bit as good-
lookin as any ae thae French actors fae France.

GABRIELLE. Well, I wouldnae say no tae Jean-Paul Belmondo.
Noo, there's a *real* man for ye!

OLIVINE. Coke . . . Coke . . . More Coke . . . Coke . . .

THERESE. Quieten doon, Mme. Dubuc!

OLIVINE. Coke! Coke!

ROSE. Aw, shut her up, will ye? Ye cannae hear yoursel pastin for
her. Shove a bottle ae Coke in her mouth, Germaine. That'll
keep her quiet for a couple ae minutes.

GERMAINE. I'm no sure if I've got any more.

ROSE. Christ, ye didnae buy much, did ye? You're really countin
your cents.

RHEAUNA (*stealing some stamps*). Och, tae hang. Three more
books'll see me get ma chrome dustpan.

ANGELINE *enters.*

ANGELINE. Hullo . . . (*To* RHEAUNA.) I've come back . . .

THE OTHERS (*drily*). Hullo . . .

ANGELINE. I've went tae see Abbé Castelneau . . .

PIERRETTE. She's feart tae look me in the eye!

MARIE-ANGE. What's she wantin tae speak tae Mlle. Bibeau for?

DES-NEIGES. I'm sure she wants tae ask her tae forgie her, an patch things up again atween them. She's no a bad soul, after all's said an done. An gie her her due, she's got enough savvie tae know how tae put things right. Things'll all work oot for the best, jist you wait'n see.

GERMAINE. While we're waitin, I'm gaunnae see how many books we've filled.

The women sit up in their chairs.

GABRIELLE hesitates, then . . .

GABRIELLE. Oh, Germaine, I forgot tae tell ye. I found ye a corset-maker. She's called Angélina Giroux. Come owre here an I'll tell ye more aboot her.

RHEAUNA. I kent you'd come back tae me, Angéline. I'm really glad. We'll pray thegither an the Good Lord'll forget all aboot what ye've done in nae time, you'll see. The Good Lord isnae spiteful . . .

LISE. Well, Pierrette, it looks like they're all pally-wally again.

PIERRETTE. Christ, would that no make ye boak!

ANGELINE. I'll jist say cheerio tae Pierrette an explain . . .

RHEAUNA. Naw, naw. Ye'd be better advised no tae speak tae her at all. Stay aside me an dinnae go near her. You're finished an done wi her for good. She's in the past noo.

ANGELINE. Jist as ye please, Rhéauna. Whatever you thinks best.

PIERRETTE. Well, that's that, eh? She's got her back in her clutches again. There's nae point in me hangin aboot here any longer nor I have tae. The whole bloody lot ae them gie me the boke, so they dae. I've got tae get the hell oot ae here an get some air so's I can breathe.

GERMAINE. Oh, that's rare, Gaby! You're a real pal! I was startin tae get desperate. It's no everybody can make me a corset. I'll go an see her next week.

She goes over to the box with the booklets. The women watch her.

Help-ma-Christ, there's no much in here! Where are all the books, eh? There's nae more nor a dozen in the box. Mebbe they're . . . Naw, the table's clear!

Silence. GERMAINE *looks at all the women.*

What's gaun on around here, eh?

THE OTHERS. Well . . . Eh . . . I don't know . . . How d'ye mean?

They pretend to search for the booklets. GERMAINE *places herself in front of the door.*

GERMAINE. Where're ma stamps?

ROSE. Come on, Germaine. Let's have a search for them.

GERMAINE. They're no in the box an they're no on the table. I want tae know here'n noo where ma stamps are!

OLIVINE (*pulling out stamps hidden in her clothes*). Stamps? Stamps . . . Stamps . . .

She laughs.

THERESE. Oh, Mme. Dubuc, hide them . . . For-Christ's-sake, Mme. Dubuc!

MARIE-ANGE. Good Saint Anne!

DES-NEIGES. Pray for us!

GERMAINE. But her claes are stuffed full wi them! What the . . . She's stowed wi them! Here . . . an here . . . Thérèse . . . Dinnae tell me this is your daein, surely?

THERESE. I swear tae God, no! I had nae idea, I promise!

GERMAINE. Show me your handbag.

THERESE. Come on, Germaine, if that's all the faith ye've got in me . . .

ROSE. Germaine, dinnae go owre the score an make a fool ae yoursel!

GERMAINE. You an all, Rose. I want tae see the inside your handbag. I'm wantin tae see all your handbags. Every single one ae yese.

DES-NEIGES. You certainly will not! I've never been sae insulted in all ma life!

YVETTE. Me an all!

LISETTE. I'll never set foot in this house again!

GERMAINE grabs THERESE's handbag and empties it. Out fall several books.

GERMAINE. Ahah! I knew it! I bet it's the same wi all your handbags. Double-crossin getts that yese are! But yese'll no get oot ae here alive! I'm gaunnae murder every one ae yese!

PIERRETTE. I'll help ye, Germaine. They're nothin but a shower ae bloody thieves! An they've the cheek tae look doon their noses at me!

GERMAINE. Empty oot all your bags!

She grabs ROSE's bag.

There . . . and there!

She takes another handbag.

There's more here. An look, still more! You an all, Mlle. Bibeau? There's only three, but jist the same!

ANGELINE. Oh, Rhéauna, even you!

GERMAINE. Thiefs, the lot ae yese! The whole gang ae yese. D'ye hear me? Yese're nothin but a pack ae thievin, bastardin getts!

MARIE-ANGE. You dinnae deserve all thae stamps.

DES-NEIGES. Aye, why you more nor anybody else, eh?

ROSE. You've made us feel like dirt wi your mullion stamps.

GERMAINE. But thae stamps are mines alone!

LISETTE. They should be for everybody!

THE OTHERS. Aye, for everyboy!

GERMAINE. But they're mines! Gie me them back!

THE OTHERS. Never!

MARIE-ANGE. There's still a lot more in the boxes. Let's help oorsels.

DES-NEIGES. Aye, why no?

YVETTE. I'm gaunnae fill ma handbag up.

GERMAINE. Stop it! Keep your thievin hands off them!

THERESE. Here, Mme. Dubuc, take thir! Here's some more!

MARIE-ANGE. Come on, Mlle. Verrette. Here's a whole lot more. Gie's a hand.

PIERRETTE. Get your hands oot ae there!

GERMAINE. Ma stamps! Ma stamps!

ROSE. Here, help me, Gaby. I've taen more nor I can carry.

GERMAINE. Ma stamps! Ma stamps!

A battle royal starts. The women steal as many stamps as they can. PIERRETTE and GERMAINE try to stop them. LINDA and LISE stay seated in the corner watching the spectacle without moving. Screams are heard, a few of the women begin to fight.

MARIE-ANGE. They're mines! Gie me them!

ROSE. You're lyin, they're mines!

LISETTE (*to* GABRIELLE). Will you let go of me! Let me go, will you!

They start throwing stamps and books at one another. Everybody reaches into the boxes as fast as they can, and they throw the stamps everywhere, even out the door and the window. OLIVINE starts moving around in her wheelchair humming 'O Canada'. A few women leave with their loot of stamps. ROSE and GABRIELLE stay a little longer than the others.

GERMAINE. Ma sisters! Ma ain sisters!

GABRIELLE and ROSE leave. Only GERMAINE, LINDA and PIERRETTE remain in the kitchen. GERMAINE collapses into a chair.

Ma stamps! Ma stamps!

PIERRETTE puts her arms around GERMAINE's shoulders.

PIERRETTE. Dinnae greet, Germaine.

GERMAINE. Dinnae you talk tae me. Get oot! You're nae better nor the rest ae them!

PIERRETTE. But . . .

GERMAINE. Get oot! I never want tae clap eyes on you again!

PIERRETTE. But I'm on your side, Germaine! I tried tae help ye!

GERMAINE. Get oot an leave me alone! I never want tae speak tae you again! I dinnae want tae see naebody!

PIERRETTE *leaves slowly.* LINDA *also moves towards the door.*

LINDA. It'll be one helluva job cleanin all this up!

GERMAINE. My God! My God! Ma stamps! There's nothin left! Nuhin! Nuhin! Ma braw new hoose! Ma beautiful furniture! All away! Ma stamps! Ma stamps!

She collapses beside the chair, gathering up the remaining stamps. She sobs heavily. Offstage is heard the others singing 'O Canada'. As the anthem continues, GERMAINE regains her courage, and she finishes the 'O Canada' with the others, standing at attention, with tears in her eyes. A rain of stamps falls slowly from the ceiling . . .

Glossary

adae	to do
ahint	behind
ain	own
ashet	pie-dish
athoot	without
awfie	awful, awfully
aye, ayeways	always
ben the hoose	in another part of the house
ben the waw fae	next door to
besom	woman (contemptuous)
bint	woman, piece of stuff
birlin	whirling
blawin	puffing, wheezing
boke, boak	vomit
braw	well, beautiful, handsome
breeks	trousers
bummin her load	boasting
caw yir pan oot	work like a horse
claes	clothes
clype	gossip, tell tales
cowped	fell, keeled, knocked over
cried	called
doocot	dovecot
fae	from
feart	afraid
flit	move
foostie	mouldy
gaun	going
gaunnae	going to
gett	git
gey lucky	very lucky
gie	give
gien	given
girnin	whingeing, grumbling
greetin	crying
guid	good
guid-sister	sister-in-law
hae	have
hame	home
haver	talk nonsense

heid	head
herlane	on her own
hoatchin	heaving, infested
hoor, hure	whore
hoor ae a lot	a very great deal
keek	peek
keelies	proles
kent	knew, known
masel	myself
messages	shopping
mind	remember
mindin	memento
mullion, mullyin	million
neb	nose
nut!	no!
nyaff	puny, insignificant person
oor	our
owre	too, over
pan-loaf	affected in accent
pechin	panting, gasping
pieces	sandwiches
rammy	argument
redd up	clear up
schuil	school
scunnerin	disgusting, nauseating, loathsome
scunnert	disgusted, bored, fed up
skail	knock over, empty
skelp	slap
skelves	splinters
snash	abuse
stoonin	throbbing with pain
taen	taken
tellt	told
teuchter	uncouth, country bumpkin
thae	those
thegither	together
thir	these
thon	that
toattie	tiny
underclaes	underclothes
vernear	almost
wean	child
went the craw road	became mentally unstable
widden	wooden, stupid
winshin	courting
yese	you (plural)
yin	one, person
youse	you (plural)

MANON/SANDRA

Characters

MANON, a young woman
SANDRA, a transvestite

Manon/Sandra, was first performed in Great Britain at the Traverse Theatre, Edinburgh, on 11 August 1984 with the following cast:

MANON Patricia Northcott
SANDRA Simon Russell Beale

Directed by Stephen Unwin
Designed by Ashley Martin-Davis

This production transferred to the Donmar Warehouse, London, on 1 October 1984.

Manon/Sandra was performed by the Nightingale Company at the Man-in-the-moon Theatre, London, on 18 July 1989 with the following cast:

MANON Jane Whittenshaw
SANDRA Mark Norton

Directed by David Oliver Craik
Designed by Lucy Burges
Stage Manager Trish Bailey
Translated by John Van Burek

In her kitchen, which is completely white, MANON, *who is very devout and all dressed in black, is rocking.*

In her 'dressing room', which is completely black, SANDRA, *a transvestite who is all dressed in white, is doing her nails.*

MANON. The solution to everything . . . is God.

SANDRA. It doesn't matter who, doesn't matter when, where or why, the answer is always to fuck.

MANON. It's true.

SANDRA. Especially not 'why' . . . 'whys' are the worst.

MANON. There's nothing you do, nothing you say that doesn't have God at the end of it.

SANDRA. Take me, for instance, I don't know why . . . about anything. And I don't want to know!

MANON. If you think about it, it's so reassuring.

SANDRA (*laughing*). Why ask yourself why, it's stupid. Especially when you can fuck, so you don't have to think.

MANON. Sometimes I try to imagine something . . . I don't know . . . just some ordinary thing, or some big thing that's very, very important, that doesn't remind me of God . . .

SANDRA. Survival by fuck!

MANON. . . . and I can't find a one!

SANDRA. Survival by itself . . . impossible. It's got to be accompanied by something . . . something enveloping . . . and warm.

MANON. And I've discovered on my own, it's true that God exists.

SANDRA. I really can't think of anything but fucking to keep me alive.

MANON. And I didn't read all that in books, either. Oh, no, I . . . I just thought about it, by myself . . . with what little I learned in school . . .

Silence.

Even if I'd never been to school, I'm sure I'd have come to the same conclusion.

SANDRA (*laughing*). Of course, not just any old fuck.

MANON. Oh, yes, I'm sure of it.

SANDRA. Nor any old piece of ass.

MANON. I'm sure . . . because it's the truth. The only one. The only truth possible. And you just have to think about it a bit to discover it.

SANDRA. Though at times . . . anyone will do the trick.

MANON. And me, I've found the truth!

SANDRA. When you get to the point where you'll take no matter what, then a fuck from no matter who will make you happy, no matter how badly he does it.

MANON. God is at the end of everything.

SANDRA. As long as it's still a fuck.

MANON. God is at the end of everything.

SANDRA. My God, you're crazy!

They both smile for a few seconds.

MANON and SANDRA. Sometimes I ask myself, what did I ever think about before I thought of that?

There is a pause. Both characters are still smiling.

I can't remember . . . I was too young.

There is a long pause, as if both characters were preparing their confessions.

MANON. I bought myself a new rosary this morning . . . It's beautiful. It's splendid! It cost me a lot of money, but I don't care, nothing's too beautiful for God.

Silence.

I don't know if I'll say it before Sunday though. It's awful . . . I'm caught between two fires and I don't know what to do . . . If I say it now, it won't count, because it hasn't been blessed yet and it would be like I wasn't praying at all . . . but on the

other hand, it's so beautiful . . . and so heavy. I bought it
'cause it was heavy. I'm sick of cheap little rosaries that weigh
nothing and look like nothing. I don't feel I'm praying any
more when I've got one in my hands . . . But this one . . .
When I saw this one, I was speechless. I was looking for a big
rosary, OK, but that big! When I saw it, I thought to myself: 'I
don't believe it, is that a real rosary or an ad for one?' . . . I
was at the Oratory, because they have the best selection . . .
and the most beautiful. So, I asked the lady if the big rosary
was for sale. 'Why, of course,' she answered, 'and I'm telling
you, it works wonders! I just got it this morning. We've only
been open an hour and already, you're the fourth person who's
asked me. Isn't it beautiful? Oh, when I saw it, my heart stood
still, no kidding. Do you know that the Mother Superior of the
Sisters of Jesus and Mary, herself, asked the price! Of course,
we'd give them a discount, but it would still be very expensive.
No, she'll probably send her chauffeur back to pick it up before
the end of the day.'

Silence.

I was so upset and excited when she said that! Then all of a
sudden, even though it was huge, I said to myself: 'I've got to
have it! I can't help it, if I see someone else buy it, I'll be so
disappointed, I'll . . . I'll . . .'

Silence.

I think maybe I almost committed a sin there, just thinking that
someone else might buy my rosary. Even the Sisters of Jesus
and Mary. Just because they brought me up is no reason to
leave them everything. Especially not my rosary. I was already
calling it my rosary . . . I asked the lady if I could touch it. At
first, she said no, because she'd just hung it up this morning
and she didn't want to spend the whole day hoisting it up and
down . . . It's so beautiful. 'Not that I'm scared it'll break,
mind you', she said to me. 'It's solid . . . and I mean solid. It's
me who's scared of breaking. The old ticker's been going too
fast for some time now . . . Oh, I do love God, but you know
what they say, to adore Him and hang around with Him all day
are two different things. I'm on my feet behind this counter the
whole day . . . I don't want to lose my job, you understand . . .
It's a good job . . . but they're pretty strict here with the ladies
that work here.' Finally, I offered to go behind the counter
myself. Well, listen, I wanted to touch that rosary. She could
see I was a serious customer, so she didn't stop me.

Silence.

It's red. Wine red. A beautiful wine red. And the crucifix is in
black wood. Oh, it's so, so beautiful. When I touched it . . .
even though it wasn't blessed, it's funny, eh, but when I
touched it, I felt like something was alive inside . . . It was . . .
warm.

Silence.

The beads are half the size of my fist . . . and when you take
four or five in your hands . . . they're heavy, and warm, and
alive.

Silence.

I didn't even turn to the lady to tell her: 'I'll take it.' I had tears
in my eyes. And I could hardly speak. I clutched the beads of a
whole decade to my chest . . . and I took a deep breath, to
keep from shaking . . . The lady said to me: 'You realize, it's
very expensive.' But I cut her off. 'I don't care.' I said it so fast
that she jumped. Then I turned to her, as if to apologize, and
very softly, told her: 'I want it. Right away. I need it. Right
away.' The lady stared at me for a minute before she answered.
It was as if she understood how I felt. Finally, she said: 'Like I
told you, I just got it this morning, so I still have the shopping
bag. I'll go and get it.' I took the rosary down myself while the
lady went for the shopping bag.

Silence.

It's not plastic. No. Plastic's light as a feather. I don't know
what it's made of. It's transparent, but it's very heavy. I can't
figure it out.

Silence.

Maybe it's God's presence that's so heavy.

Silence.

When I'd gathered it all in my arms . . . I was so happy, I
didn't know what to do next. There I was, stuck behind the
counter with this big red rosary hanging all over me . . . I burst
out laughing! I laughed so hard! I laughed, I laughed! People
were staring at me and the more they looked, the more I
laughed. Finally, I was so weak, I had to lean on the counter.

Silence.

But I settled down.

Silence.

The lady came back with the shopping bag and the two of us put the rosary inside. It barely fit! The lady was amazed when I told her I'd pay cash. Her eyes as big as saucers, she said: 'Aren't you afraid to walk around with all that money in your purse?' 'Oh, no,' I said, 'my Guardian Angel is with me and God's armed him like a soldier to protect me from wicked people.' Boy, did she laugh. I always make people laugh with my comparisons. I picked up my big package and caught my two buses home. A little boy on the 129 thought it was a set of blocks. But his mother told him: 'Why no, Raymond, can't you see, it's a big rosary. Look at the nice wooden crucifix, isn't that lovely?' Then she asked me: 'Is it for a church, Sister?' I went all red. It's not the first time that I've been mistaken for a nun, but it's the first time someone thought that I was carrying things for the Church! 'No,' I told her, 'it's for me. It's my rosary.' And with that, the lady starts laughing like a maniac. 'For the love of God,' she says, between a couple of hiccoughs, 'what're you gonna do with it, skip rope?' Well, I wasn't gonna stand for that! 'I'll have you know, lady, rosaries like this are made for people like you!', I screamed at her, right there on the bus, 'for people with near-sighted souls!' That shut her up. But she didn't look like she understood. People can be so thick when they decide that they want to be stupid. Well, too bad for her! I didn't even tell her I wasn't a nun!

Silence.

But still, that doesn't solve my problem. I must admit, I'm a little embarrassed to show up at the parish house with my shopping bag to get it blessed. I should have had it blessed when I bought it, but I was too excited. I was too anxious to see how it would look in the place where I wanted to put it. No, I'll wait until it's blessed before I start praying on it. It's a sacrifice. I'll offer to God for the sins of that crazy lady who understood nothing and who laughed at me on the bus. I'll pray for her on my little rosaries and wait to pray for myself on the big one.

SANDRA. I know someone who's gonna cream his jeans tonight. Ah, and if he doesn't like it, he can go jerk off!

Silence.

I really don't know what came over me . . . The things you do
sometimes, it's weird . . . You're just sitting around, as usual,
doing the same old things, as usual, bored up the ass, as usual,
not thinking about a thing, when all of a sudden: pow, flash!
An idea! You ask yourself where on earth that came from . . .
Then you go on being bored up the ass trying to get it out of
your mind. And you can't.

Silence.

That's what happened to me when I woke up around five this
afternoon. I gazed lovingly on my splendid alabaster body,
finding it a bit tiresome because I've known it for a few years . . .
My fine, supple little hands that shake a bit 'cause I smoke too
much, but which are still full of life, knowing, experienced,
perverse; my darling little tootsies, wide as a barge, that usually
smell like a German shepherd, but which I always manage to
disguise as a classy French poodle, trotting lightly but firmly
around the bed; my thighs, too muscular for a woman, but
which know how to loosen up when the time comes; my arms,
ah! my arms; wings . . . No, how can I say? Feathers! And not
ostrich, but swan's! My arms, downy before, steel wool during
and merciless after!

Silence.

But especially, I gazed upon my super-duper queen-sized
dickie, so gorgeous, erect like a towering inferno, prepared like
a boy scout in search of a good deed.

Silence.

If I didn't keep him in check, Dickie would help little old ladies
cross the street! I said to myself: 'You're aging well, old girl,
you're aging well.' No flabby folds on the tummy yet, the
wicked fairy still hasn't touched your luscious thighs with her
cellulite rod . . . and you're approaching the middle of your
life. I'd even say you're standing on the threshold. Bravo,
bravo, bravo! So, for my reward, I took myself on a Cook's tour
of the premises, and paused lovingly at the most sensitive spots.

Pause.

Afterwards, I wiped my hands on the sheet. Well, all that's very
nice, but there are times you wake up, eh, and even if you
know you're still tempting, there's this empty feeling inside . . .
As if . . . something's missing.

Silence.

I got up to eat. Wof! Eat's a big word! I nibbled on a melba
toast, with no more appetite than I chew my nails when I'm
having my chimney cleaned by a trick with no talent . . . What's
more, my Nescafé tasted like chewing tobacco, never mind if
I've never chewed the stuff, let alone seen it. Really, everything
was all wrong. What do you expect when you have your
morning erections at five in the afternoon, your life is upside
down. Anyway, I found myself languishing in front of the
mirror like I always do when I'm depressed. And that's when
the lights went on. The minute I saw myself in that three-faced
mirror that reminds me of all my friends, I don't know what I
did . . . a look that I gave or a sweep of my swan's feathers . . .
but it cut through my head like a meat cleaver: I saw my cousin
Hélène when I was a little girl, though still a boy, standing at
my Aunt Robertine's dresser, putting on green nail polish! To
drive her mother crazy, I guess. Maybe she thought it looked
good too, you never can tell. Anyway, she didn't get the idea
from *Good Housekeeping* or *Châtelaine*. Not in 1952! I remember it
was so ugly! Especially the green lipstick! Then . . . isn't it
crazy . . . I felt like doing the same thing. Oh, it's hardly
original, I know, fat Laura's been wearing black lipstick for
three weeks because her Siamese cat that everybody hates was
murdered with some liver pâté truffled with arsenic or old lace,
or God knows what, by her own girlfriend, Jos Trudeau, who'd
had it up to here with those two crooked eyes howling in his
ear! But as for me, dressing up for the sake of dressing up . . . I
don't like that. 'Everything to turn 'em on, nothing to turn 'em
off,' that's my motto. But I had such a craving all of a sudden
to do something crazy . . . Can you believe it? . . . Green! Why
green? I can't even stand a red the least bit deep, what with my
capricious complexion . . . I went back to bed and told myself
it would all blow over . . . Nice try, sugar plum. I could already
see the look on my Caribbean siren's face when he caught sight
of me with a green suck-hole. A Mwatiniquais is vewy
suspicious. He'd pwobably think I caught some tewible
Wagnewian disease! 'The Twilight of the Sods!'

She bursts out laughing.

'The Twilight of the Sods!' That's a beauty! I'm gonna put that
in my repertoire! I doubt Cwistian would get it though.
Anyway, I tried to go back to sleep; no way. I rolled it over on

one side, then I rolled it over on the other, nothing doing . . .
By this time, I'm seasick, so I climbed out of my dinghy and
jumped into my pants. 'I can always try to find some,' I said to
myself, 'who knows if they even make it any more?' Hoping I
wouldn't find any, I stepped outside my palace of a thousand-
and-one torrid nights and . . . They had some at the corner
drugstore! Mind you, this is no Tamblyn's. The owner is in her
sixties, a jerk of an ex-priest, married to an unscrupulous
travelling salesman. Which means that between the two of
them, they'd flog their mothers for fifty cents and give you
change. You walk in the door and pussy-face has dollar signs in
her eyes and a bag marked 'International Pharmacy' in her
hand. But this time, I figured I'd plug her up proper, and not
where you're thinking, 'cause wrecked convertible priests are
not my department. I just said, like this, very matter of fact:
'One "Avocado Sea" lipstick please and a nail polish to match,
natch.' 'Right away, Sandra dear', he says, without raising an
eyebrow. How could he, he doesn't have eyebrows. And he
pranced away behind his shelves of rat poison and other
concoctions. I was, to say the least, dumbfounded. After two
minutes and three seconds, this would-be has-been of a nun
shows up with a tube of green lipstick and a bottle of green nail
polish. They were neither Revlon nor 'Avocado Sea,' but they
were green! And her, the sow, she was pink with pleasure! She
flashed her aggressive dentures and cooed: 'Do come and show
me the effect.' Effect, my ass! I could have shoved my fist up
her Anus Dei, all the way to the elbow. But she wouldn't even
notice, she's too used to it. I sure didn't feel like dressing up as
an overripe avocado after that! A few shrimps and a Thousand
Island dressing and I'd look like an entrée in a chic restaurant!
Oh, but pride, what will we not do in thy name?

Silence.

I always assume responsibility for my actions, so here I am
obliged to plaster my nails and kisser with green shit! I can tell
already, the flies will love me tonight. But why do it if I don't
want to any more . . . Sandra, don't ask why!

She smiles.

Besides, maybe I still want to, just a weenie bit . . . Just to see
the incwedible look on Cwistian's face!

She bursts out laughing.

Never ask yourself why. Go ahead and do it. Life is too short.

She stops laughing.

As a matter of fact, it gets shorter every day . . .

MANON. I put it in my bedroom. I placed it in the hands of the life-sized statue of the Blessed Virgin. It's so beautiful, I . . .

Silence.

I don't deserve such happiness. That's what I told myself as I walked down the street this morning. I had the shopping bag in my hand and I was so happy I almost felt guilty. When I turned the corner of the alley, I saw there were still some empty garbage cans that people hadn't taken in yesterday. One of the cans was knocked over, so I stopped.

Silence.

I think that's so dirty, garbage cans lying in the middle of the alley. Even if they're empty.

Silence.

I picked it up.

Silence.

And without meaning to, I glanced in at the bottom. There was an old missal stuck to the bottom, along with potato peels and carrots. A missal, in a garbage can . . . with the thought that had just gone through my head that I wasn't worthy of such joy. Right away, I thought, it's a signal from God. I knew it . . . I didn't deserve my rosary. And God wanted me to sacrifice my beautiful rosary, so beautiful, that cost me so much, to help him save the sins of the world. My rosary had to go into the garbage with the missal . . . as an offering! It was a great honour . . . but so hard to do! My beautiful red rosary! And I'm not rich . . . I saved up a long time to buy that! I looked all around. No one. I took a deep breath . . . I didn't want to . . .

Silence.

But there was the missal, stuck to the bottom . . . in the garbage! Someone else had already made her sacrifice!

Silence.

Slowly, I lifted the bag and lowered it into the can. I had to lean in.

Silence.

It smelled awful.

Silence.

All of a sudden, I burst out: 'You know, God, sometimes You ask me to do the hardest things', I said to God: 'But here, You're the boss, so take it.' The bag just fit in the garbage can. I said to myself: 'I guess that's where it belongs'. Then I couldn't take any more and I burst into tears. I hadn't cried so hard for years. I leaned on the garbage can.

Silence.

I cried so hard my tears fell into the bag.

Silence.

All of a sudden, Mme. Quenneville's little boy, who I didn't hear coming, shouted behind my back: 'So, you're a garbage picker now? You ought to be ashamed! You must be awful hungry!' And he burst out laughing. A real devil's laugh! I was so insulted that without even realizing it, I picked up the bag, shoved the little brat against the wall and ran into the house. I locked myself in, closed the Venetian blinds and threw the rosary at the feet of the Blessed Virgin in the corner of the room. 'Your Son asks too much of me,' I said, really mad, 'at times, He goes too far. This rosary belongs to You. They always told us when we were little that every rosary in the world belongs to You, so here, take this one, too, keep it for me . . . and try to intercede for me please. I'm afraid that was too big a sacrifice for my little soul.' I got down on my knees and touched every bead, one after another. Oh, not praying, it's not blessed yet, but I wanted to go over it once to see . . . just to see. And . . . that calmed me down . . . completely. In the time it took me to go once around, the Virgin Mary had settled everything with her Son. When I got to the crucifix, which I'd saved till the end, I wasn't sure if I should touch it. I said to myself: 'If I haven't been pardoned, it'll burn me like fire.' But I had faith. I put my hands close to Our Lord's body, I touched Him with the tip of my finger. It was just lukewarm. Like the rest. Oh, the warmth was still there, like in the store, but now it was even more comforting. The warmth of God, not the heat of the Devil. For a long time, I held my hands on the body of Our Lord who suffered so much for us . . . when all of a sudden . . .

Silence.

I felt this need . . . I felt this terrible need to kiss him . . .

Silence.

I couldn't understand . . . I had the crucifix in my hands and
. . .

Silence.

All of a sudden, I started kissing the body of Our Lord, as if it
were the last thing I would do in my life. I was sure I was going
to die after . . . be struck down! What joy! What pure joy! Like
bubbles of happiness bursting in my heart . . . and I could
hardly breathe! I stayed prostrate for a long time. When I
finally got up, I was completely at peace. I understood
everything that had happened to me . . .

Silence.

God wanted to test me like He did Abraham when He asked
him to kill his little boy in the story of the burning bush. God
asked me to sacrifice what was dearest to me in the whole
world and I did it! Yes, I did it! Like Abraham, I raised the
knife against my most precious possession. I put God Himself
into the garbage! And it wasn't the Devil that God sent to me,
no, the Quenneville kid was His voice. My own burning bush!
It was His way of saying, 'You've done enough, Manon, go
along home now and be happy!'

Silence.

I wish everyone could understand the workings of the world
like I do. But most people don't know how to interpret the
messages.

Silence.

Only a few of us understand.

Silence.

I hung the rosary on the hands of the Blessed Virgin and I got
into bed . . . The Blessed Virgin and I smiled at one another.
Then . . . slowly . . . I fell asleep.

SANDRA. I hope it smears. I wonder if they still make real
lipstick that smears, like in the old movies. So kinky, to run my
green lips over his black body . . . What colour would that

make? A lean sinewy body zebraed in green . . . My God, I'm getting a hard-on! I can't wait!

She smiles.

One thing's sure, this'll be his first green blow-job!

She laughs.

I'm almost tempted to put some up my ass, instead of K-Y.

Silence.

They'd be right then, the ones who say I'm rotten to the core! A green anus! Sandra the Martian!

There is a long silence.

I'll ask him to stand next to the TV, naked. He's got these incredible buns. I'm gonna . . . I'm gonna open my green lipstick and write stuff on his back . . . Every insanity that comes into my head. God knows that won't be hard. Secret graffiti, hermetic signs I wouldn't dare put on toilet walls for fear someone, someday, would recognize my handwriting and spread it all over town that 'no one's as low as Sandra!' The shameful thoughts you write on your lover's back are the only graffiti that can really shock and besmirch those who come after you. Who would dare repeat a secret read on someone's back?

Silence.

Next, I'll draw circles on his bum, like targets. His cheeks like green targets with two black dimples . . . Softly, I'll run my tongue between the two green targets. It will taste dark. I'll scrawl on his legs, his belly, his chest, his face . . . green signs that only I can understand. I'll write a pornographic book on his body. My own Bible. The Book of Genesis according to Sandra the Martian. The Pentateuch, the Song of Songs, the Old Testament and New Testament according to Sandra the Green. And above all, the Apocalypse according to me!

Silence.

Then I'll take whatever's left of my green lipstick, crush it in my hands and anoint his sex with green blood. My hands . . . will be green with sticky blood . . . I'll stand back a bit and I'll say to him: 'Open yourself wide and let me read!'

Silence.

Then I'll wipe it all away. I'll smear everything I've written to keep it for myself! Those who'll come after me are not deserving. I won't stoop to insult them. I'll rub . . . I'll rub until his skin and the green lipstick merge completely. I'll knead him, I'll oil him, I'll massage him with the green blood of Sandra the Martian. Next, I'll take out my cream-satin sheets, my beautiful sheets that cost me a fortune, that I never use 'cause they're too cold and too slippery . . . I'll have him lie down on my cream-satin sheets. He'll be nailed to the middle of my bed . . . crucified with green glue. I'll close the sheet over him, drawing the four corners to his navel.

Silence.

I want to have a green imprint of the first Black God.

Silence.

I'll kneel beside the bed. If silence could invade the world! The street deserted, the television off, the radios dead, the babies bloated with pablum, the parents stuffed with chips and Coke, dozing before their own stupidity. To say nothing. Hear nothing. Only to wait. For the green of my blood to bleed from his skin into the cloth. Let it take time.

Silence.

Time enough to mummify him.

She smiles.

Yes, that's it, from now on, I'll mummify my lovers. All those who stick their noses in here hoping to stick their cocks up my ass will end up in the closet, hung up on hangers like old dresses we never throw out in case we lose weight again, or in case we put it back on. Dresses we know we'll never wear again, but we also know no one will ever wear again. No one will ever again go out this door to strut his triumphant virility in the small of someone else's back!

Silence.

I'm sick of being for them what they are for me . . . one among many. A number! A three-star fuck . . . or two-star . . . or one-star. A gourmet meal or a bowl of slop. Seventh heaven or the fifth basement. I want to be last. The last one to award the stars. The last one with the right to put the mark of quality on a piece of ass, like the stamp on a ham.

Silence.

When my collection starts taking up too much room, I'll turn them into lamps! I'll stick a shade on their heads and I'll pull their dicks to make them light up. Starting today, I'll electrify my lovers so they can throw a bit of light on the amorous thrashings of their successors.

She bursts out laughing.

We should teach our children to dream awake and out loud. It beats masturbation and it doesn't make a mess!

Silence.

When Cwistian gets a load of my unripened kisser, he'll probably get scared and turn tail like a rabbit. And I'll be left standing here with my greening plans. Unless of course, it turns him on and he throws himself at me before I've even time to tell him he's liable to end his days out on the balcony, stuffed with straw, with a turban on his head, a lantern in his hand and billiard balls in place of eyes.

Silence.

A beacon on my balcony, lighting the way to heaven for all the pilgrims in search of a fuck.

Silence.

Of the two possibilities, I don't know which I like best. Instant rape by Speedy Cwistian can be pretty humiliating, but he's so beautiful . . . I think I'd rather look at him than fuck him. But I'm afraid beauty never lasts, even in green lipstick. Which means . . . thank you! Next! Maybe it's just as well he gets scared and runs. I'll take a last look at his fabulous ass and his legs long as organ pipes.

Silence.

Que sera, sera, eh?

Silence.

This green really is ugly!

Silence.

Hey, wait a minute, the clap is green too! My God, my lover's on his way here and I'm dressed like the clap!

MANON. I had a dream. It's strange to say because usually I
never dream. I read once somewhere that it's not normal, not
to dream. That it's dangerous. But I don't believe that stuff. It
never worried me not to dream. Dreams are bad. Dreams are
something you can't control and things you can't control are
bad. And the proof is: the dream I had this morning was bad. I
must have been too tired . . . or too upset over what had just
happened.

Silence.

And now, I'd give anything to forget it.

Silence.

If only I'd forgotten it the minute I woke up.

Silence.

I'll do all I can to forget it . . . but now . . . it hasn't been long
enough yet. But I'm going to forget it! I'm going to forget it!

Silence.

When I was small, we had a neighbour who was crazy,
hysterical, and she'd scare me . . . A real maniac who'd do all
she could to shock people. She was beautiful, but frightening,
like a fallen angel. I think that's what she was: a fallen angel
that God sent to remind us that hell exists and sometimes it's
not far away . . .

Silence.

I remember once I'd gone to ring their bell because I used to
play with her cousin, Michel . . . He was my best friend . . .
And she came to the door . . . I'll never forget it. She'd put on
green lipstick that day, and I think her nails were green, too . . .
Yes, yes, her big devil's claws! I turned and ran back home,
tumbling down the stairs . . . I was screaming: 'The devil, the
devil, I've seen the devil!' My mother took me in her arms and
told me it was true. That Hélène was the devil. We both got
down on our knees and prayed for her . . . no . . . no . . . we
didn't pray for her . . . we prayed to God that he'd get rid of
her as fast as he possibly could. Her and her whole family? We
hated them all, the whole gang! Except Michel. I loved Michel.

Silence.

I still hear her laughing, the demon.

Silence.

The demon with the green mouth.

Silence.

It was that laugh that came back to me in my dream . . .

Silence.

I was lying on my bed, just as I was when I fell asleep . . . I was still looking at the statue . . . Dear God . . . will You never forgive me?

Silence.

Why did You send me that sign? Why have You upset me even more than this morning?

Silence.

The statue's lips and finger nails were green. It was her. Hélène. The fallen angel. With the same smile, the same gentle smile as the Virgin Mary . . . but with her own eyes. Those crazy eyes that would burn me when I was little and she'd come down from their place and watch us play, me and her cousin. 'Not too close to the balcony,' she told us once, 'you might be tempted to crawl underneath and play doctor like we all did at your age.' Demon! Demon!

Silence.

In my dream, the statue was still clutching the rosary . . . But she held it . . .

Silence.

It was dirty, the way she held it. They weren't the hands of the Virgin Mary, held open like cups . . . These hands were closed around the beads. She was rubbing the beads as she looked at me with her crazy eyes . . . I started to scream and the statue dropped the rosary on the floor.

Silence.

She came towards me . . . I was so scared, I screamed! I screamed! I screamed: *Vade, retro, Satanas!* Then all at once, the Virgin Mary . . . no, not her, the other one . . . Hélène . . . the statue . . . I don't know any more . . . The woman who's damned and all painted green threw herself on me and she was saying things . . . things . . . they were so gentle!

Silence.

Yes, it was gentle.

Silence.

And it was good. She touched me all over, just like I'd touched the body of Our Lord, and she whispered to me: 'Do you like that, Manon? Do you like it? It's nice, isn't it? Would you like to feel my lips on your body, all over, on your skin, eh, like you were doing a while ago? You want to know what He feels when you caress Him, when you kiss Him? You want to feel how good it is? Eh?' I was crying, I was pleading. She began to caress me all over! 'No,' I said, 'no, Hélène, don't do that, that's ugly! It's a sin! It's dirty! That's not the way I do it! That's not why I do it!'

Silence.

'I never did it for that! I swear it!' She stopped caressing me and said: 'I'm not Hélène! I'm not Hélène! Don't you remember me? Don't you know me? We were the same age . . . we were born the same day . . . we played together in the yard in front of the house. I'm dressed like the rest of them, but it's me. Don't you recognize me?' For a second, I took him in my arms and held him tight, tight, tight . . .

Silence.

Michel! Michel! Why did you become like her? She was crazy! Look what you've become! A degenerate!

Silence.

She screams.

Why have You done this to me? Why so much in one day? Why do You put him back on my path, that little boy I loved so much and who's followed his sick cousin into hell! Why didn't You send me a dream filled with Your presence instead of that other one? Why were her caresses so good for me? It's for You that I sacrificed my life! My whole life!

Silence.

She speaks very quietly.

When I woke up, I was soaked with sweat. And . . . Oh! The statue was in its place, but the rosary was on the floor. One of the hands was broken.

Silence.

And You know how much I believe in signs! In the signs You so often send to comfort me, to test me, or sometimes just to remind me You're still there, beside me, omnipresent . . . beneficent . . . protective . . . fatherly! If You start sending me signs I don't
understand . . .

Silence.

She speaks louder.

If You start sending me signs *I don't want to understand*, I'm warning You, You won't fool me! I will not understand them! If You get too demanding, just remember, I can make demands too! I believe in You because You exist, but also I believe in You because You're good! Because You have to be good! The dream You sent me today wasn't good! And I'm sending it back! You made me commit a sin while I was asleep . . . You hear me? . . . I was asleep!

She screams.

I couldn't defend myself!

Silence.

I'm sorry. Perhaps You're right. I'm sorry. Forgive this poor soul . . . this poor lost soul . . . a poor confused soul . . . Forgive me. Forgive me.

Silence.

Take me back. Back to Your heart. Take me back. Take me back. Take me back to Your heart.

SANDRA. Sometimes it just comes over me . . . Doesn't matter what I'm doing, I have to drop everything. Just before I plunged into my green paint a while ago, it hit me . . . And when it happens, it's pointless to try to resist. I ran to my mirror, took off all my clothes and slopped my puss with make-up remover . . . I scrubbed and scrubbed, I think I used up two boxes of Kleenex, Man Size. I wiped my face completely away. I pulled my hair back with an elastic.

Silence.

I have the honour to officially declare that of the man I was not a single trace remains. Nothing! However much I looked, dug,

examined . . . I could not find myself. My own face has ceased
to exist. Completely vanished beneath the tons of make-up to
which I have subjected it, vanished behind the dozens, the
hundreds of other faces I've drawn in its place . . . When I
remove my make-up my eyes disappear, my mouth shrinks, my
eyebrows move, my cheeks puff up . . . and none of it goes
together. The hundred other faces of women that I've drawn,
that I've created myself, look more like me than what's left
underneath.

Silence.

To find myself naked in front of a mirror, exactly as Mother
Nature created me, gives me vertigo of nothingness. I don't
exist any more.

She smiles.

The only thing that's still me . . . the only thing that's still the
same . . . oh, it's matured well, 'cause it's hung around so
long . . . it's grown in experience, 'cause it's lived life to the
hilt, it's even been forgiven for having loved too much . . . the
only thing I've never disguised . . . that's right, is my cock. Its
appetites are the same, its demands are the same, even its
illnesses, little head colds or serious diseases, the shameful
ones, the runny ones, the ones that give pimples, they haven't
changed. I have . . . remained my cock. The rest is only
accessory. The rest is fabrication, an invention to lure into a
thousand nameless traps the thousands of victims my cock is
lusting after with his appetites voracious and his instincts
ferocious. I'm not a woman by taste, I'm not a woman by need.
My cock is merely a piece of go-between meat at the service of
a gluttonous crotch! My cock commands; me, I obey! A slave?
Of course! Such a beautiful word. Full of promise. Lies.
Cunning. Twists. But at times, enormously gratifying. I am the
slave of my senses.

She bursts out laughing.

When I'm neither on the prowl nor fucking, I'm not alive. The
rest is filler. Everything I'm saying now is filler. Between my
Martiniquais this morning before he went off to work and my
Martiniquais tonight when he gets home from work. Me, I'm
for action! No words. Pure. Speech is a venomous act, but
fucking is a stream of honey flushed out from under cover,
spread out in bright sunlight and savoured in the white burst of
silence.

There is a long silence.

I found my masquerade for today. While doing my first nail a while ago, I found the face that the variable Sandra will don tonight. I have decided it will be the Virgin Mary herself who will receive a Martiniquais in her bed tonight. A new role. A new composition. The Mother of us all. To play the role of our Mother in the arms of the ascending race. To submit oneself to the Black, to yield to Him, sacrifice to Him, the purest, the most sacred image of our degenerate civilization.

Silence.

I'm gonna dress up like the life-sized statue that screwball next door bought after a fire destroyed part of the church in our parish. A statue bought in a fire sale. What an image! It's the statue of the Virgin Mary picked up in a fire sale that will get it in the ass tonight with the gigantic wang of the victorious Martiniquais! I'll stand in the corner of my room in my white dress, my blue cape and my little gold belt . . . Yes, I'll stay standing the whole time! He'll lift my dress from behind. I won't move. My arms open. The frozen smile. But green! My eyes fixed, empty, turned in upon the ravaged saint. Saint Sandra the Green of the Fire Sale!

There is a long silence.

I am the Immaculate Cuntception! And it's tonight the Black Sparrow of the Holy Ghost will pay me a little visit . . . to bring me the Big News . . . And the Big News is that the New Messiah will be one very weak baby!

MANON. I have always followed Your instructions to the letter. Even if it meant great sacrifice. And You were never too shy about asking for those! I saw You at the end of all my suffering because You made me realize that You were present everywhere and I accepted every misfortune with pleasure *in order to be with You!*

Everything in my life centres on Your presence! I wanted to become a nun at one time. You didn't want me to, so I didn't. I hope You remember at least. When I was a teenager, that was my greatest wish, my most beautiful dream. To take Communion with the other nuns in the infinite pleasure of Your presence. And there was nothing to stop me . . . I was all alone here, my mother and father were dead . . . and my sister . . .

Silence.

My mind was almost made up when You forbade me to do it.
Do You remember that afternoon? You told me Yourself, inside
me. You softly, but firmly murmured in my ear that my place
wasn't there, but here. In my mother's bed, in my mother's
life . . . You ordered me to perpetuate my mother who was a
saint . . . even though it cost me dearly, even though I cried for
days, because, for me, the convent was the very picture of
happiness in communion with You . . . even if *I* thought I
belonged in a convent, I stayed here for You! You've given me
ample compensation since, that I won't deny . . . For fifteen
years, You have given me enormous joy and my gratitude is
even greater still . . . but . . .

Silence.

She speaks softly.

You don't come to see me so often any more. I don't feel Your
hand on my hand or on my head like before . . . Now, I need
ten times the energy, ten times the concentration to finally feel
Your breath in my soul. Before, I had only to think of You and
Your breath would carry me off. You'd come right away and
the two of us would smile and float away, leaving everything
behind us, You, Your golden throne where a crowd of saints,
each more important than the other, waited on You, prostrate,
passive, submissive . . . and me, my rocking chair, with my
potatoes to peel and my carrots to shred. It didn't take two
seconds, then hours would pass and neither of us would even
notice . . . You said so Yourself!

Silence.

Entire days we'd spend together between heaven and earth,
while You'd explain the world to me in a way I could
understand and forgive it, and I'd listen to You, on the verge of
fainting. And I'd tell You that everything that You do is done
well, that You are perfect, and that I must have been the
luckiest person in the world to have found You. You made me
happy, perfectly happy for fifteen years!

There is a long silence, then she explodes.

I have a right to my pleasures! I have a right! I'm used to them
now! I like what You did for me and I want it to continue! You
don't just ask a poor girl to sacrifice herself for fifteen years and

then drop her! I have to coax You now with rosaries the size of watermelons and go through your Holy Mother in order to reach You. Does that seem right to You? And again, today, I still haven't succeeded. I haven't felt Your presence for a second! It's the first time that's ever happened!

Silence.

Can't You see I need You? I'm on the verge of blasphemy. If one day goes by, one single day, that You don't come to see me, I'm warning You, I'll go crazy and then I'll be capable of anything! I know, lately I'm tired sometimes . . . it's hard for me to meet You halfway . . . but couldn't You make a little effort? I sincerely believe You are everywhere at all times, but that little bit of Yourself You give to me alone, what's become of that? You've given it to someone else. A new soul who's fresh and more available . . . already! No, that cannot be! You can't cheat me like that, walk away as if You didn't need me any more! If . . . if You abandon me, I'm capable of plenty, you know! If You abandon me, Satan is not far away and I could easily go find him myself, before He even thinks of throwing himself at me!

Silence.

If You don't come right away, I'm lost.

Silence.

It wasn't You. I know it wasn't You who sent me that dream a while ago . . . You know as well as I do there's a part of me that would like nothing better than to throw itself head first into the great abyss! So make up Your mind! It's Your choice! Me, I let myself go! It was always You who made the decisions, don't stop now. It was always You who took my fate in Your hands, so I'll tell You once and for all, it's Your responsiblity! I wash my hands of it and if I lose myself, then it's You who loses me!

There is a long silence.

She closes her eyes.

Ah! . . . Ah . . . yes . . . finally . . . I feel it . . .

She smiles.

I feel You coming . . . yes, yes, closer . . . come closer and I'll forgive You for everything! Oh, for the love of me, where were

You? I gave You my life . . . give me my share of Yours! Haaa . . .
yes . . . take my hand . . . take me away . . .

SANDRA. When I finish my nails, I'll go sit on the balcony and
wait for Cwistian. I'll keep doing my number, perpetuate my
role of comic transvestite for all the neighbours who must
already be waiting for me, wondering what I'll come up with
today.

Silence.

They accepted me pretty fast around here . . . without ever
knowing who they were dealing with.

There is a long silence.

I moved back to Fabre Street right across from the house where
I was born.

Silence.

When I saw the ad in the paper two years ago, I couldn't
believe my eyes. A sign from heaven! I trotted right over,
disguised as a quiet, young stenographer, yet another of my
dazzling compositions. The landlord never had a clue, my
handwriting's illegible! So . . . ever since then, I've been
watching Fabre Street live, all over again. I returned to my task.

Silence.

In no time at all, I was friends with most of the women. Of
course, they knew right away I wasn't a real woman. They'd
never seen a number like me up close.

Using different voices.

'How do you do it?' 'Why do you do it?' 'Did you have an
operation?' 'Don't ever let me catch you sniffing around my
husband!'

Silence.

What they don't know is that this variable woman, this
character who's so funny and so original, who they've grown
used to seeing wiggle down the street with men of all ages, all
conditions, all colours and all beautiful . . . is little Michel who
lived in the house across the street twenty-five years ago. For
some of them, a childhood friend, the baby of that crazy family
of twelve, all piled into the same house, that made so much
racket for everyone else.

Silence.

It's incredible how little Fabre Street has changed. Just aged a bit. But not changed. Not at all. At least half my childhood friends, especially the girls, have stayed here, married here and had kids that look like us. At times, it's as if I can see our gang playing out there in the alley . . . while the girl next door, with whom I played doctor a quarter century ago, knits beside me as she tells me things I know almost better than she, about her childhood, which, by the same stroke, is also mine; our games, our joys, our boundless happiness to be small in the fifties . . . and noisy . . . and Masters of the World!

Silence.

To have been a child on Fabre Street is a privilege that leaves an indelible trace.

Silence.

I suppose it's the same for everyone else, except I wasn't there.

Silence.

Obviously, no one recognized me, but most of the girls came back to me, like before, to tell me their troubles, saying afterwards, without fail: 'You really understand us, don't you, us women?'

Silence.

Yes, I do.

Silence.

Now they say: 'It's because you're queer', while before they'd say: ''Cause you take the time to listen to us.'

Silence.

To think that that's when they were right.

Silence.

Sometimes I want to come right out and tell them: 'Hey, it's me, look, remember me? I was the leader of your gang! It's me who organized the picnics at Parc Laurier and Parc Lafontaine. It's me who made myself a Batman costume and haunted the alleys at night to scare you. If only you knew. If only you knew how it's me who was scared. I pretended to be brave and you thought I was brave. I pretend to be a woman and you think I

am a woman. I've always fooled you because I had to, but if
you only knew . . . if you only knew how much I love you!

Silence.

But I would never tell them that.

Silence.

There's only one of them I've never dared speak to again . . .
When I first saw her . . . I'd just moved in that morning and
I'd decided to eat on the balcony, 'cause the house was a mess.
I saw her turn the corner, all bundled up in her old maid's
outfit, her hair pulled back, her eyes to the ground, looking at
the tips of her shoes, her little waddle of a walk, like an
embarrassed nun . . . Manon . . . Manon, my sister . . . my
twin . . . Manon, who was born the same day as I, almost to
the hour, to whom I gave all the passion I possible could; her
twin, born of a different mother, but exactly like her . . .
Manon, my antithesis, my contrary, forever clinging to her
mother's skirts, a false saint, dry as a prune, while I gravitated
around my enormous mother, generous to a fault, suffocating
as a dog day . . . Manon, whom I would like to have taken in
my arms, to kiss her, caress her and say: 'What has become of
you . . . Look at me, I'm the shame of society', laughing and
clapping my hands.

Silence.

But . . . the minute I saw her, I knew she was impregnable,
inviolable, inapproachable, smooth as a stone, slippery as moss,
cold as an ice-floe. Impossible to touch. Like her mother. When
her mother would see me, she'd say: 'That child is a sin!'

Silence.

For two years, I've watched Manon dry up like a raisin and I've
never, never dared speak to her. She doesn't know I'm here.
My mere presence would kill her. I am the negation of her life.

Silence.

Of her Faith.

Silence.

If what people tell me about her is true and it probably is true
– she's my twin, I feel her, I know her, she's me – if all that is
true, I envy her! People who are happy are so rare.

She laughs.

When I feel like crying, I go and stick my nose to the window and stare at Manon's closed Venetian blinds. Sometimes a faint little light, yellow, almost dirty, sneaks out through the metal strips, the bars of her prison. The light of a flickering candle. The light of a dying heaven and a rising hell. And I tell myself: 'Manon has just left on one of her long journeys towards day'.

Silence.

I have found someone truly happy whom I can watch live her happy, mouse-like life, surrounded by the decor of my own happy childhood. And I am reassured. About everything.

Silence.

If Manon had not existed, I would have invented her.

MANON. My head has wings. My mind is like a bird cage with the doors wide open. All my thoughts fly out of me at once. Like sparrows set free. Everything flows from me. I am emptying out, I destroy everything in my path. My thoughts pulverize Fabre Street and I stand amidst the ruins like a rising spring . . . Not too fast! Not too fast! Too fast is no better. Don't take me too high, too soon. Wait for me! If I get dizzy I'll fall and I'll have to start over!

Silence.

Ah! I've found my wings again! I'm soaring! In Your vast shadow! You shield me from the sun because its light is evil. Only Your light which seeps into the darkest night, the most secret shadows, which tears the soul as blows from a sabre, pierces the eye, bursts it, opens and revives it, only Your light which bites the skin and leaves the mark of wounds, only Your light which explodes the truth, the only truth, Your truth, only Your own light is good. The only one possible. The only one liveable. You have humbled Yourself to give me an infinitely small particle of it, which kills me. Your truth crucifies me. I find, at last, supreme joy in Your shadow, sheltered from all defilement. I follow You like a speck of dust, yet I glow like a comet.

Silence.

I am . . . a speck of gold dust in the eye of God!

Silence.

Ah! Higher! I'm ready now! Higher! Crush me beneath Your weight. Make of me a thing deformed, twisted, but holy; let me limp in the fringe of Your will!

Silence.

Let me obey!

Silence.

Give me Your hand, I can't see You now. I can't feel You any more! Don't leave me like this, alone in the void. I feel like I don't exist.

Silence.

Hurry, come take me, I feel that I only exist inside someone else's head! Don't let me fall back. If I do, it's not my own body I'll find. If You let me fall, my lips and my nails will be green. Help me! Help me deny my body! As long as possible! Give me back my wings! Give me back my wings, I'm falling!

She screams as if she were falling.

Ah!

She opens her eyes and bursts into tears.

What have I done to be punished so! What have I done to be punished so! Take me back with You, You are all I have left in my life. You are the answer to everything . . . in my life! I've destroyed all doubt . . . my faith is all I have left. All I have left are the rewards offered by my faith in You. All I have left are the rewards I offer myself for my faith in You. I believe in You. So You believe in me! Even . . . if . . . I have . . . been . . . invented . . . by . . . Michel.

SANDRA. Go on, Manon . . . climb!

MANON (*as if she were flying away*). Ah . . . ah . . . thank You! I knew it! I knew it! Thank You, dear God! Thank You!

SANDRA. Climb . . . higher . . . climb!

MANON. Yes . . . higher!

SANDRA. Keep going . . . right to the end! Go to the end of your journey! Climb! Climb! Climb! And take me with you! I want to leave!

She screams.

Take me with you, because I don't exist either! I, too, have been invented! Look, Manon! Look! His light is coming!

There is very intense light for five seconds, then a blackout.

ALBERTINE IN
FIVE TIMES

Characters

ALBERTINE AT 30
ALBERTINE AT 40
ALBERTINE AT 50
ALBERTINE AT 60
ALBERTINE AT 70
MADELEINE

Albertine in Five Times was first performed in Great Britain at the Donmar Warehouse, London, by the Tarragon Theatre, Toronto, on 7 September 1986. The cast was as follows:

ALBERTINE AT 30	Susan Coyne
ALBERTINE AT 40	Clare Coulter
ALBERTINE AT 50	Patricia Hamilton
ALBERTINE AT 60	Jay Coghill
ALBERTINE AT 70	Doris Petrie
MADELEINE	Diana Belshaw

Directed by Bill Glassco
Designed by Astrid Janson
Lighting by Harry Frehner
Translated by John Van Burek and Bill Glassco

ALBERTINE AT 30 *is sitting on the verandah of her mother's house at Duhamel in 1942.*

ALBERTINE AT 40 *is rocking on the balcony of the house on la rue Fabre in Montreal in 1952.*

ALBERTINE AT 50 *is leaning on the counter of the restaurant in parc Lafontaine in 1962.*

ALBERTINE AT 60 *is walking around her bed (in the house on la rue Fabre) in 1972.*

ALBERTINE AT 70 *has just arrived at a home for the elderly in 1982.*

MADELEINE *has no age. She acts as confidante to the five Albertines.*

ALBERTINE AT 70 *enters her room at the home for the elderly. She speaks in short, choppy sentences, almost singing. She has that carefree tone of someone returning from afar. A sprightly little old lady.*

ALBERTINE AT 70. Mind you, they're probably right . . . I'll be better off . . . much better. Hard to believe, eh . . . If someone had told me this a year ago . . . (*She runs her hand over the bed.*) The bed's a bit hard . . . not as bad as the hospital though. The sheets look clean. (*She goes to close the door.*) I don't know if I'll ever get used to this smell. (*She comes back to the bed.*) I'll put my television there . . . so when I sit in my chair I can see fine. Actually, they planned this pretty well. It's small, but they thought about it. It's their job, eh, to figure it out.

She puts her purse on the bed and takes off her coat, which she neatly folds, setting it down beside her purse. She straightens her skirt a bit.

There, I'll be more comfortable. I mean, from now on, this is home. (*She sits in her chair.*) This was the first thing I tried when I came to look at the place. It's as important as the bed, eh, a good rocker!

She rocks for a few moments. ALBERTINE AT 30 *steps out onto the verandah of her mother's house at Duhamel. She's a bit plump, but very pretty. She is wearing a light summer dress, circa 1940. She sits in a rocking chair and rocks to the rhythm of* ALBERTINE AT 70. *The latter notices her and stops rocking, as she lets out a little cry of surprise. They look at each other and smile.* ALBERTINE AT 30 *gives a little wave.* ALBERTINE AT 70 *gives herself a good push and starts rocking again.*

ALBERTINE AT 70. I've come back from a long way off. Six months ago, I was dead. It's true! They cracked three ribs reviving me. (*She laughs.*) Crazy, huh? Every time I think of it I can't help laughing. Though it's hardly funny. But what the heck, it's better to laugh than whine about it till you die . . . a second time . . . next time for good, I hope! (*She laughs.*) Not many people can say they've died twice, that's for sure! Mind you, after my second time, I won't be telling anybody anything. I doubt if you come back from the dead more than once. Anyway, when I go back again, I'll be very happy to stay. I've no wish to spend the rest of my days making trips like that. I've never been further than Duhamel in my life!

She looks at ALBERTINE AT 30, *who laughs in turn.* ALBERTINE AT 40 *comes out onto her balcony on la rue Fabre. She's a little fatter than at 30. Her face is harder. She is wearing old clothes, clumsily patched up. At the same time,* ALBERTINE AT 50, *jovial, singing, and skinny as a rail, plants herself at her counter. She wears a belted dress and her hair is dyed black. She has brought with her a toasted bacon lettuce and tomato sandwich, upon which she chomps away.* ALBERTINE AT 70 *watches her while she rocks.* ALBERTINE AT 30 *seems lost in her thoughts.*

ALBERTINE AT 70. When I woke and saw myself with all those tubes and bandages and transfusions . . . believe me . . . I felt like going right back where I came from. And when they told me I'd be dragging around for months on end with all that pain . . .

ALBERTINE AT 60 *comes in, stooped, aged, pale. She goes to her bedside table and takes a pill from a plastic container without even checking the label.* ALBERTINE AT 70 *sighs in exasperation and shifts her chair, turning her back to her.* ALBERTINE AT 60 *looks at her and shrugs, sits on her bed and rocks from side to side. For a few moments the five* ALBERTINES *sit silently.*

ALBERTINE AT 70. Mind you, now that it's over, I'm glad to be back.

The other four look at her.

Because things are better. I've got peace. Because here I'll be fine. (*Brief silence.*) Even if I don't like the smell.

MADELEINE *comes out onto the verandah of the house at Duhamel.*

ALL FIVE ALBERTINES. Ah, Madeleine!

MADELEINE *smiles.*

ALBERTINE AT 70. Hello!

MADELEINE. Hello!

ALBERTINE AT 70 & 30. Come and sit down . . .

MADELEINE *sits beside her sister on the verandah of the Duhamel house.*

MADELEINE. Night falls fast here, doesn't it?

ALBERTINE AT 30. I've never seen anything so beautiful.

Silence.

ALBERTINE AT 70 *leans forward a bit to hear them better.*

ALBERTINE AT 30. Never. It was red, and yellow, the sky, then green . . . It never stopped changing.

Silence.

ALBERTINE AT 70 (*moved*). The country . . .

ALBERTINE AT 30. The sun dropped like a rock behind the mountains . . . Just before it disappeared the birds stopped singing. Completely. It was like everything, not just me, was watching the sun go down. In silence.

ALBERTINE AT 70. You talk funny . . .

ALBERTINE AT 30 *turns to her.*

ALBERTINE AT 30. What?

ALBERTINE AT 70. The way you talk, there's something funny . . .

ALBERTINE AT 30. Hmm . . . It's true, I don't often talk about nature. But if you'd seen that, it was so beautiful! When the sun disappeared, the birds, the crickets, the frogs started their racket again, all of a sudden, as if someone turned on a radio. (*Silence.*) In the city . . . (*Silence.*)

ALBERTINE AT 70. The country . . . God, it was beautiful that night!

ALBERTINE AT 30. In the city, you never see that . . .

ALBERTINE AT 70. Oh no . . . In the city, everything's hospital grey . . .

ALBERTINE AT 30. Sometimes when I look out the kitchen window I can see that the sky's a yellowy-orange, then pink, then lemon-yellow, but the sheds get in the way. I can't see what's going on . . .

ALBERTINE AT 50. I can see it.

ALBERTINE AT 30. And I don't have time. In the city I never have time for things like that.

ALBERTINE AT 50. I take the time!

ALBERTINE AT 70 *laughs.*

ALBERTINE AT 50. It's true! When I finish work sometimes, at night, six o'clock . . . parc Lafontaine is so beautiful.

ALBERTINE AT 30. Not like the country . . .

ALBERTINE AT 50. Of course, not like the country, but so what? In my whole life I saw the country for one week! No point harping on that. No, today, I take what comes. And if it's a big beautiful sunset, I stop and I look at it.

ALBERTINE AT 70. You talk funny, too.

ALBERTINE AT 50. What do you mean, I talk funny?

ALBERTINE AT 70. I don't know . . . I don't know. It's like you use words I never used . . .

ALBERTINE AT 50. I talk like I talk, that's all . . .

ALBERTINE AT 30. Maybe it's 'cause you don't remember . . .

ALBERTINE AT 70. Don't kid yourself . . . I remember . . . I remember everything . . . For the last few months that's all I've had to do, is remember . . . But it seems to me I never talked nice like that . . . But don't stop . . .

ALBERTINE AT 50. It'll be hard not to stop if you're going to make us talk badly!

ALBERTINE AT 70. You don't have to talk badly, that's not what I said . . .

Brief silence. The three ALBERTINES *look at one another.*

But maybe you're right . . . I was brought up to think that everything about me was so ugly, I'm amazed to hear I said something beautiful.

Brief silence.

MADELEINE (*to* ALBERTINE AT 30). I brought you some hot
  milk. It'll help you relax. In his letter Dr Sanregret says you
  should have some before bed . . . It was a bit hot, I've let it
  cool . . .

ALBERTINE AT 30. That's good of you, thanks . . .

MADELEINE. But I hope it's not cold . . . If it's cold,
  it's no good. Tell me if it's cold, and I'll heat up some more
  . . .

ALBERTINE AT 50. Madeleine!

MADELEINE. Yes?

ALBERTINE AT 50. I haven't had milk for ages. Nowadays, it's
  coke.

MADELEINE. You don't need it anymore . . .

ALBERTINE AT 70. I have it sometimes before I go to bed . . . It
  reminds me of you, Madeleine . . .

They look at one another.

I miss you, you know . . .

ALBERTINE AT 50. Milk plugs you up . . . Coke delivers!

ALBERTINE AT 30. Look, Madeleine, there's still a patch of
  green. If you look at it for a while it turns blue, but when you
  look next to it, out of the corner of your eye, you can see it's
  green.

She lifts her head to look at the sky. ALBERTINE AT 50 *and* 70 *do
the same.*

ALBERTINE AT 30, 50 & 70. There are so many stars in the sky!

ALBERTINE AT 30. And I had to land here, where everything's
  wrong.

MADELEINE. Where did you want to land?

ALBERTINE AT 30. Madeleine, do you believe there are other
  worlds?

ALBERTINE AT 40. There'd better be, 'cause this one's no great
  shakes!

The others look at her.

ALBERTINE AT 40. Why look at me like that? You think this one's bearable?

ALBERTINE AT 60. Hell no!

ALBERTINE AT 70 (*sharply*). You be quiet!

ALBERTINE AT 60. What's the matter?

ALBERTINE AT 70. I don't want to hear you, that's all . . .

ALBERTINE AT 50. Why do you talk to her like that?

ALBERTINE AT 70. Never mind! Finish your sandwich.

ALBERTINE AT 50. I've finished my sandwich!

ALBERTINE AT 70. Then finish your coke.

ALBERTINE AT 50. I've finished my coke!

ALBERTINE AT 60. Then finish your squabbling! I'm tired : . .

ALBERTINE AT 60 *turns to her for the first time.*

ALBERTINE AT 70. If you don't shut up . . .

ALBERTINE AT 60. What will you do, eh?

ALBERTINE AT 70. I know, I can't do anything. Proof is you're there!

ALBERTINE AT 60 *blows her nose.*

ALBERTINE AT 60. Everybody hates me!

ALBERTINE AT 70. No wonder!

ALBERTINE AT 50. Stop treating her like that!

ALBERTINE AT 70. It's clear you never knew her.

She looks at ALBERTINE AT 60 *for a few seconds.*

Pathetic!

ALBERTINE AT 40. Well, when they announce their first trip to the moon, or the sun, I'm going to buy me a one-way ticket, pack my little bag, and I'll be happy as a clam.

ALBERTINE AT 30 *and* 50 *and* MADELEINE *laugh.*

ALBERTINE AT 50. And what in God's name would you do on the moon?

ALBERTINE AT 40. I don't know what I'd do, but I sure know what I'd leave behind.

ALBERTINE AT 30. I wonder if they'll ever make it to the moon . . .

MADELEINE. There's nobody on the moon . . .

ALBERTINE AT 40. Lucky for her!

ALBERTINE AT 70. Yeah, they'll make it there, but it won't change much for us . . .

ALBERTINE AT 60. That's hogwash . . . Do they think we're idiots? I saw them land on the moon, on television . . . Who're they trying to kid!

ALBERTINE AT 50. If they showed it . . .

ALBERTINE AT 60. Don't believe everything they show you!

ALBERTINE AT 40. Mind you . . .

ALBERTINE AT 60. Who was there to film them, eh? We saw the two of them, prancing around like gazelles . . . there was no third guy to make the movie! So how come we could see them?

ALBERTINE AT 30. Maybe they had automatic Kodaks . . .

ALBERTINE AT 60. Kodaks? Boy, are you behind the times! They've got these huge buggers now, you should see them . . . You'd never get them on the moon, not in a hundred years!

ALBERTINE AT 70. Stop talking nonsense . . .

ALBERTINE AT 60. Do you believe them?

ALBERTINE AT 70. Yes . . . now I believe them . . .

ALBERTINE AT 60. What made you change your mind?

ALBERTINE AT 70. I've changed a lot . . . I've read stuff. Now I've got new glasses, I can see, I keep informed. I understand things.

ALBERTINE AT 60 *shrugs.*

That's right, don't bother to think, shrug your shoulders, that's all you ever do!

ALBERTINE AT 60. Say what you like, when they give us that crap about trips to the moon and the stars, I switch channels. I'm not kidding, I'd rather watch cartoons and I hate them!

There's a bloody limit! And if it's my money they're after, they better not hold their breath! It'll be a cold day in hell before they get a penny from me to build their movie sets and their deep sea costumes to make us believe they're exploring other planets for the good of the human race! Ha! There's enough misery here without looking for it elsewhere! I tell you, when my first pension cheque arrives in the mail, I'll be waiting on the doorstep, and not one of those buggers is going to touch it!

ALBERTINE AT 40. Mind you, too few people's no better than too many. And it's cold on the moon, I don't like being cold . . .

ALBERTINE AT 50. Far as I can tell, you don't like much.

ALBERTINE AT 40. Wrong, I don't like anything!

ALBERTINE AT 30 (*lost in her thoughts*). I could sit here and rock till . . . (*She smiles ironically.*) No point in saying till when, eh, that'd be dumb.

MADELEINE. Stay longer . . . We're here till September. Uncle Roméo's letting us have the house till the kids go back to school. Then he'll close it up for the winter.

ALBERTINE AT 30. One or two more sunsets won't change my life . . . Besides, when I get home, I won't see them anyway . . .

ALBERTINE AT 50. Get 'em while you can . . .

ALBERTINE AT 30. And I can't spend my life watching the sun go down behind a mountain.

ALBERTINE AT 50. Why not?

ALBERTINE AT 30. If you've got all that free time, good for you . . . I don't. I've got la rue Fabre waiting for me.

ALBERTINE AT 40 (*close to tears*). La rue Fabre, the kids, the family . . . Dear God, I'm fed up . . .

ALBERTINE AT 30. The kids, the family . . .

ALBERTINE AT 60. Who gives a shit about the family!

ALBERTINE AT 70. The kids . . . God knows where they are today . . . Mind you . . . I do know . . . I know all too well.

MADELEINE (*after a silence*). You hear that?

ALBERTINE AT 70. I've survived everyone . . . and it's not even interesting.

MADELEINE. Whip-poor-wills. We get them every evening.

ALBERTINE AT 50. I saw a bird wedding a while ago . . .

ALBERTINE AT 30. They sure looked like they were having fun.

ALBERTINE AT 40. I think they were swallows . . .

ALBERTINE AT 30. . . . but I'm not certain . . . I don't know about birds. But they were blue . . . and they gulped their food.

ALBERTINE AT 40. Is that possible? Swallows in the city? I thought swallows were country birds . . .

ALBERTINE AT 60. Who gives a shit about swallows!

ALBERTINE AT 30 *takes a deep breath.*

ALBERTINE AT 30. It smells so good it hurts!

ALBERTINE AT 70. Breathe again.

ALBERTINE AT 30 *takes another deep breath.*

Tell me . . . tell me what it smells like . . .

ALBERTINE AT 30. I couldn't say . . . I don't have words to describe it . . . it's too good!

MADELEINE *gets up, goes toward* ALBERTINE AT 70, *who looks at her intensely.*

MADELEINE. It smells of freshly cut hay . . . cow dung too, but just a bit, enough to say it's there . . . It smells of all the flowers that throw off their perfume before going to bed . . . It smells of water, muck, the moist earth . . . It smells green. You know, like parc Lafontaine when they've just cut the grass. Sometimes you're right in the middle of a smell and all of a sudden, just because you move your head a bit it changes . . . then there's a new smell and you're so surprised you stop breathing so you won't lose it . . . But it's already gone and another smell has replaced that one . . . You can sit there on the verandah all evening and count, yes count, the number of different smells that come to visit. (*Silence.*) It smells of life.

ALBERTINE AT 70 *puts her hand over her mouth to keep from crying.*

ALBERTINE AT 70. In the hospital, all you could smell was medication. It was like the other smells were . . . hidden. Except when someone else in the room was sick, but that's understandable . . . Mind you, we were all sick . . . Me too, at first I guess . . . I doubt if I smelled too good . . . but at least I'd apologize. Nobody could say I wasn't polite! The others . . . Well, a lot of them were pretty confused, eh? . . . They put me on the floor with the confused, I never did figure out why . . . I mean, I never lose my head . . . Anyway . . . the smells always got covered up sooner or later by the medications or the bleach . . . 'Cause it was clean, I can't deny that. But here . . . When I came to visit the first time, I thought . . . I don't know . . . that it smelled bland like this 'cause someone had just been sick . . . But when I came back today it smelled the same. And yet, it seems clean here too. (*She seems to have a sudden moment of panic.*) What if it always smells like this?

ALBERTINE AT 50 *puts down her sandwich.*

A brief silence.

I guess after I've lived with it for a while, I won't notice it any more.

MADELEINE *offers her the cup of milk.*

MADELEINE. Here. Drink your milk. It's going to get cold.

ALBERTINE AT 70 *takes the cup and drinks.*

ALBERTINE AT 70. Tastes like the country.

MADELEINE. You'll sleep better tonight.

ALBERTINE AT 70. I hope so. You see, it's my first night . . . naturally I'm a bit nervous . . .

MADELEINE. It's real cow's milk, not like in the city. The farmer brings it every morning with cream so thick you can stand a spoon in it.

MADELEINE *takes the cup away.*

ALBERTINE AT 30. Not like the city, you can say that again . . . In the city, milk like that, they'd call it cream!

MADELEINE *comes back to* ALBERTINE AT 30. *Troubled,* ALBERTINE AT 70 *watches her go.*

ALBERTINE AT 50. Here it smells of french fries. Everywhere. All the time. Even my hair and clothes smell of french fries! Before I go out at night though, I put on perfume. I don't know what you'd call a mixture like that, but I like it. I smell good. And strong!

ALBERTINE AT 40. Here it smells like a bunch of people who don't belong together . . . Bickering, jealousy, hypocrisy . . .

ALBERTINE AT 60. Must smell like a tomb in here. I don't dare open the window though, I'll catch my death . . . I've shut myself up in the house where I was born . . . hell . . . in one room of the house . . . to protect myself from the smell outside. Nothing can touch me now, I've lost my sense of smell.

ALBERTINE AT 70. It smells of death in driblets. Did I go through all that to end up here?

The others look at her. She blows her nose.

It'll be better tomorrow.

ALBERTINE AT 60. You think so?

ALBERTINE AT 70. Yes, I think so!

MADELEINE *hands the cup of milk to* ALBERTINE AT 30 *who drinks it slowly.*

ALBERTINE AT 60. I have no memory of any smells. Not even the pines that made me so dizzy when I arrived at Duhamel. All my life, from then on, when anyone mentions smells, I can see myself standing there on the verandah, filling my lungs with that air! Now . . . (*She looks at* MADELEINE.) . . . you could spend hours trying to describe that smell to me and I wouldn't remember it.

ALBERTINE AT 30. Mother's old cup . . .

ALBERTINE AT 70. Mother?

MADELEINE. It's all worn and stained, but not chipped. Sort of like a new antique.

ALBERTINE AT 70. Who mentioned mother?

ALBERTINE AT 30. I did.

ALBERTINE AT 70. I haven't thought of her in ages.

ALBERTINE AT 40. Lucky you!

MADELEINE. Strange to think our mother was born right here.

ALBERTINE AT 30. Yes. Somehow the house is full of her.

ALBERTINE AT 40. Well I sure think of her! I can't help it, she's on my back all day long!

MADELEINE. Yet she left here a long time ago. It's funny, we never knew her in this house, but she spoke of it so often, missed it so much, you'd swear she'd forgotten something here, that she'd only just left . . . Sometimes I open a door and I have the feeling she just walked out of the room . . . I want to run after her . . . Crazy, huh?

ALBERTINE AT 30. She never should have moved to the city . . . We'd be country folk today, and a lot better off. (*Silence.*) Madeleine, I don't want to go back to the city!

ALBERTINE AT 60. The city . . . the country . . . what's the difference!

ALBERTINE AT 40. I can't stand her any more . . . and it's mutual.

ALBERTINE AT 30. I know it's impossible, and my kids need me, even if they're terrified of me, and it's only a week's rest 'cause I'm tired . . .

ALBERTINE AT 40. But it's almost over . . . thank God.

ALBERTINE AT 30. So tired, Madeleine!

ALBERTINE AT 50 (*to* ALBERTINE AT 40). It's terrible to talk that way about your own mother!

ALBERTINE AT 30. So tired!

ALBERTINE AT 40. I know it's terrible. But that's what I think . . . and it's none of your business.

ALBERTINE AT 50. Why not? She's my mother too! I know I always fought with her, but I don't remember wishing her dead!

ALBERTINE AT 40. Well I'm reminding you. When she's gone, we'll be rid of her, you especially.

ALBERTINE AT 50 (*finding her old aggressive spirit*). How can you say such things?

ALBERTINE AT 40 (*in the same tone*). Weren't you relieved when she died?

Silence.

ALBERTINE AT 50. I wish I'd never been like you!

ALBERTINE AT 40. I wish I wasn't going to smell of french fries!

ALBERTINE AT 60. When she died in her sleep, like a frail little bird . . . it threw me . . . (*Silence.*) A hole. Empty.

ALBERTINE AT 50. Like something missing . . .

ALBERTINE AT 60. Yeah, that's right, something was missing . . . I was going round the house in circles . . . looking for it . . . And one day I realized that what I was missing was her insults. She always . . . fed me . . . with her insults . . . and I missed them . . . 'cause she no longer released what was inside me, like before.

MADELEINE (*to* ALBERTINE AT 30). Forget all that, the city, mother, your problems. Enjoy your vacation. Empty your head. (*Silence.*) Finish your milk.

ALBERTINE AT 30 *finishes her milk in one swallow.*
ALBERTINE AT 70 *makes the gesture of lifting the cup to her lips.*

ALBERTINE AT 70. You've brought back the cup!

ALBERTINE AT 60. But I filled the hole. I just took mother's place and passed the insults on to Thérèse.

ALBERTINE AT 30 *sets her cup on the floor, gets up, and stretches.*

ALBERTINE AT 30. How am I going to sleep with all that racket?

MADELEINE. I know, they make an awful noise. The crickets are the worst. They go on all night. But it's funny, that's what finally puts me to sleep . . .

ALBERTINE AT 40. She thinks I'm stupid . . .

MADELEINE. Then the frogs wake me up again.

ALBERTINE AT 30 *smiles.*

ALBERTINE AT 40. Mother's always thought I'm stupid . . . You all think I'm stupid, don't you?

MADELEINE. Come on, where did you get that?

ALBERTINE AT 40. I see you, you know . . . and I hear you! Poor Bartine this, poor Bartine that, she doesn't understand, but it's not her fault, she's so stupid . . .

MADELEINE *moves a little toward* ALBERTINE AT 40.

Well, I may not be too bright, Madeleine, but I've got eyes and ears.

MADELEINE *has come to sit beside* ALBERTINE AT 40.

MADELEINE. You know what you're like, Bartine. Some of the things you say and do make no sense at all.

ALBERTINE AT 40. Madeleine, I've got a son who's not normal and my daughter's a wildcat but that doesn't mean they get it from me! My husband was also there when I made those kids! Sure, none of you talk about him, he disappeared long ago, he was a war hero who did us proud, how could he be anything but perfect! But you all forget one thing: he was a moron! He was the idiot, Madeleine, not me. Who else but an idiot would go and get himself killed for nothing on the other side of the ocean? I bet you anything he ran right out in front of them playing the hot shot, and there's no way he died a hero, he died a buffoon. A buffoon! He was a buffoon, Madeleine! But it's me who's here, me, so it's easy to judge me!

MADELEINE. I never said you were crazy or wild or that your kids get it from you . . .

ALBERTINE AT 40. Baloney! You all decided long ago I wasn't intelligent. Just because I don't understand things your way doesn't mean I'm not intelligent. There's more than one kind of intelligence, you know. The rest of you . . . you're intelligent with your heads but you refuse to accept that someone can be . . . I don't know how to say it, Madeleine . . . With me it's not my head that works, it's . . . it's my instincts, I guess. I know I do things without thinking, but I'm not always wrong, am I? Ever since I was a kid people give me these funny looks whenever I open my mouth because I say what I think . . . You condemn what I say, but you don't hear yourselves! You ought to use your heads less and your hearts more. And you never listen to me! The minute I open my mouth I get this look of contempt that's so insulting! You're so convinced I'm a jerk you don't even listen to me any more.

MADELEINE. Why do you say that . . . What am I doing now?

ALBERTINE AT 40. Sometimes you enrage me, Madeleine, with your superior airs!

MADELEINE. Oh, don't start that again . . .

ALBERTINE AT 40. Sure, I know, I'm supposed to put up with it
and say nothing, but the minute I speak everyone shits on me.

MADELEINE. What do you expect, you're impossible! We can't
say a word to you, you start swinging, you don't think!

ALBERTINE AT 40. There you go, just like mother!

MADELEINE. I don't know what mother says . . .

ALBERTINE AT 40. Madeleine, that's a lie!

Silence.

You see, you can't answer . . .

MADELEINE. How can you answer someone as stubborn as you!

ALBERTINE AT 70. Poor Madeleine . . . I put you through the
wringer, didn't I . . . but I wonder if you knew how much I
loved you . . .

MADELEINE *looks at her.*

MADELEINE. No. We never knew if you loved us or hated us
. . . so often you said you hated us. To each of us in turn, or all
of us together . . . At times that's all we got from you, we could
feel it, almost touch it.

ALBERTINE AT 40. You don't know what it's like, to feel alone
in a house full of people! Nobody listens to me because I'm
always screaming and I'm always screaming because nobody
listens! I don't let up from morning to night. By noon I'm
exhausted. I run after Marcel to protect him, and I run after
Thérèse to stop her from getting into worse trouble than the
day before. And I yell louder at mother than she yells at me!
I'm fed up, Madeleine, fed up with always being in a rage! I'm
smart enough to see your contempt for me, but not clever
enough to shut you up!

MADELEINE. Don't shout, Bartine! Try to speak in a softer
voice . . .

ALBERTINE AT 40. I can't . . . My heart is bursting with things
that are so ugly, if you only knew . . .

Silence.

ALBERTINE AT 50. It will pass.

ALBERTINE AT 60. Yeah, but it'll come back . . .

ALBERTINE AT 40. And when you come strutting in here with your whiz kids and your perfect husband . . .

MADELEINE *puts her hand on her sister's arm.*

MADELEINE. I don't 'strut' in here, and you know it . . .

ALBERTINE AT 40. Come off it! If you can find fault with everything I say and do, I can do likewise. You come here to shove your happiness under my nose, make sure I'll get a good sniff! Your oldest is always top of the class, Thérèse is a waitress in some dive. Your youngest is funny as a monkey; meanwhile Marcel retreats more and more into himself.

MADELEINE *gets up.*

Don't run away!

MADELEINE. Trying to talk to you when you're like this is hopeless. You won't listen . . .

ALBERTINE AT 40. Seems we all have that problem . . . When it's my turn to speak, it's never interesting, is it?

ALBERTINE AT 50. I'm getting sick of you . . .

ALBERTINE AT 40. That's right, take their side too!

ALBERTINE AT 50. I'm not, but you're talking in circles.

ALBERTINE AT 40. And I suppose they're not?

MADELEINE. It's impossible to talk to you. You can't control your temper! The number of times I've sat with you, trying to have a discussion . . . Within five minutes all hell breaks loose, we're ready to kill each other . . . every time!

ALBERTINE AT 70. If you'd taken another tone with me I might have been capable of discussion.

MADELEINE *looks at her.*

MADELEINE. You agree with her?

ALBERTINE AT 70. You bet!

ALBERTINE AT 40 (*suddenly*). The first time someone's understood me!

ALBERTINE AT 70. 'Cause you went about it all wrong . . . (*to* MADELEINE.) You know what I wanted you to do, Madeleine? No, not what I wanted, I don't think I wanted it . . . but what you should have done.

MADELEINE. What?

ALBERTINE AT 70. It wasn't discussion I wanted . . . we had this day in and day out . . . no, I needed you to put your arms around me, to hold me . . .

ALBERTINE AT 50 (*softly*). I haven't been touched by anyone for so long.

ALBERTINE AT 40. That's not true. That's not what I needed.

ALBERTINE AT 50. Oh yes it is!

ALBERTINE AT 40. Are you judging me too? Is that it? You know better than me what I need?

ALBERTINE AT 70. We're not judging you . . .

ALBERTINE AT 50. . . . we remember.

ALBERTINE AT 40 (*to* MADELEINE). Keep away from me!

MADELEINE *approaches her and takes her in her arms.*

MADELEINE. I didn't know, Bartine . . .

ALBERTINE AT 40. Don't touch me! Leave me alone!

They remain frozen for a moment. Nothing moves on the stage.
ALBERTINE AT 40 *has kept her eyes wide open, as if terrorized.*

MADELEINE (*very gently*). Relax . . .

ALBERTINE AT 40. I can't.

MADELEINE. I hug my own kids all the time. I should have realized. But with a sister who's always in a rage, it's not so easy . . . Relax . . . let yourself go . . . Think . . . think of Duhamel, ten years ago . . . Remember how beautiful it was?

ALBERTINE AT 40. You won't get me with sentiment! My rage is too great.

ALBERTINE AT 60. At times, I sort of remember . . . physical contact. I mean my head remembers. And it's so revolting. I thank my stars I don't know a soul any more.

ALBERTINE AT 30. Madeleine?

MADELEINE. Yes?

ALBERTINE AT 30. What did Dr Sanregret say in his letter?

MADELEINE. Well, he said you should rest 'cause you've had a bad shock.

ALBERTINE AT 40 *pushes her away.*

ALBERTINE AT 40. If I took a rest every time I had a bad shock, I'd have spent my life in the sanatorium!

ALBERTINE AT 30. Did he tell you everything? The whole story?

ALBERTINE AT 40. Are you kidding, the whole world knows my problems. That's all they ever talk about.

MADELEINE. I don't know what happened, Bartine. There's no electricity here . . . no telephone . . .

ALBERTINE AT 40. Goddamned liar! I've got you now! You get a letter from Dr Sanregret who sends you this letter to tell you I need a rest 'cause I've had a bad shock, and he doesn't even tell you what it was! You take me for an idiot?

ALBERTINE AT 30. Did he tell you I almost killed Thérèse?

The others look at her.

MADELEINE. No . . . He says you gave her a beating, but . . .

ALBERTINE AT 40. Don't believe her!

ALBERTINE AT 30. I want to believe her. I want to get it off my chest!

ALBERTINE AT 40. Why bother? She'll only despise you more . . .

ALBERTINE AT 30. Madeleine, I almost killed Thérèse.

ALBERTINE AT 40. That's right, confess! Trust her. It's your funeral. You'll have the whole family laughing behind your back.

MADELEINE (*to* ALBERTINE AT 30). Aren't you exaggerating . . .

ALBERTINE AT 30. If Gabriel hadn't arrived, I think I would have killed her.

ALBERTINE AT 40 (*to herself*). Maybe you should have. I wouldn't be screaming on my balcony right now, like some nut in a strait-jacket!

ALBERTINE AT 30. I have this huge force inside me, Madeleine.

I have a power in me, that scares me. (*Silence.*) To destroy.
(*Silence.*) I didn't ask for it. It's there. If I hadn't been so
miserable, I might have forgotten it or conquered it, but there
are times . . . times when I feel . . . this rage, yes, rage.
Madeleine. I'm crazy with rage. (*Silence. She lifts her arm a bit.*)
Look . . . the size of that sky. That whole sky couldn't contain
my rage. (*Silence.*) If I could explode, Madeleine . . . But I'll
never explode . . . Not after what I did to Thérèse. I'm too
scared.

MADELEINE. You want to tell me about it? . . . It might help.

ALBERTINE AT 40. You're dying to know, aren't you? There's
no phone, but there is one in the village! And it won't be long
before mother knows everything!

MADELEINE. Stop interrupting all the time. If I'm such a liar
don't talk to me. Don't phone me ten times a day to complain;
don't come bawling to our place three times a week . . . Decide
one way or the other, Bartine. Either speak your mind, or never
speak to me again! (*Silence.*) Your accusations are ridiculous!
(*Silence.*) You're not so important that we spend our time spying
on you . . .

ALBERTINE AT 40. Then leave me alone! Forget about me.
Pretend I don't exist!

MADELEINE. Sure, and in two days you'll say we abandoned
you!

ALBERTINE AT 40. Ah, go to hell, the lot of you!

MADELEINE *moves away from* ALBERTINE AT 40 *and sits on the
edge of the verandah at Duhamel.*

MADELEINE. You don't have to tell me . . .

ALBERTINE AT 70. It's so difficult!

ALBERTINE AT 30. You'd think we were alone in the world, just
the two of us . . .

ALBERTINE AT 70. It's so dark all of a sudden . . .

ALBERTINE AT 60. Makes you want to whisper . . .

ALBERTINE AT 40. No, makes you want to destroy everything!

ALBERTINE AT 50. The moon's not up yet. The full August
moon is always late.

ALBERTINE AT 30. From down there on the road, the house must look like a lantern. I wonder if someone going by could see us here . . . From that distance they probably couldn't tell I'm a criminal, eh? (*She closes her eyes.*)

ALBERTINE AT 40. They don't need binoculars to see that.

ALBERTINE AT 30. If you only knew, Madeleine, it hurts so much. (*Silence. She opens her eyes. She sighs.*) One week off. A week's rest. Then it starts all over again . . .

MADELEINE. It's our role, Bartine . . .

ALBERTINE AT 30 *suddenly turns to* MADELEINE.

ALBERTINE AT 30. Our role! It's not our role. It's our lot!

She sits in the rocker again.

ALBERTINE AT 70. Shhh . . . not so loud. Think before you speak.

ALBERTINE AT 30. I know, your lot's better than mine, but . . . don't you feel . . . don't you feel you're in a hole, Madeleine, a tunnel, a cage?

ALBERTINE AT 60. A cage . . . Ah, yes . . . a cage.

MADELEINE. I don't know what you mean, Bartine . . .

ALBERTINE AT 60. In a cage! You know what that is, a cage!

MADELEINE *turns to her.*

With bars! Bars, Madeleine, that keep you from getting out! Because it's you who's in the cage!

ALBERTINE AT 70. You asked for it!

ALBERTINE AT 60. That's not true!

ALBERTINE AT 70. Look at yourself! A cage is all you deserve!

ALBERTINE AT 30. In ten, twenty years, we'll still be here, in our cage with bars. And when we're old, when they don't need us any more, they'll put us in cages for old women. And we'll go crazy with boredom!

ALBERTINE AT 70. No, that's not true . . .

MADELEINE. What makes you think this way all of a sudden, Bartine?

ALBERTINE AT 70 (*a little stronger*). Not true!

ALBERTINE AT 30. I don't know. (*Silence.*) I don't know. It's not like me to rebel.

ALBERTINE AT 60. Rebel?

ALBERTINE AT 70. If I'm here, it's not because they don't need me any more . . . it's because I'm alone.

ALBERTINE AT 30. I guess what's happened has really thrown me . . .

ALBERTINE AT 70. All alone. Like a dog!

ALBERTINE AT 60 (*ironically*). To rebel?

ALBERTINE AT 40 (*to* ALBERTINE AT 30). Talk about your rage.

ALBERTINE AT 30. What?

ALBERTINE AT 40. Talk about your rage!

ALBERTINE AT 60. It never does any good to rebel . . .

ALBERTINE AT 70. No, I mustn't give in to despair . . . Help me!

ALBERTINE AT 50 *goes over to* ALBERTINE AT 70. *She gently takes her hand.*

Thank you.

ALBERTINE AT 60. It's childish to rebel. The punishment is always too great.

ALBERTINE AT 30. It's my rage, Madeleine . . . my rage wants to strike out . . .

ALBERTINE AT 60. And when the rage comes back . . .

ALBERTINE AT 30. But I don't know how, or where, or at whom!

ALBERTINE AT 60. Words . . . can't describe . . . the impotence of rage.

ALBERTINE AT 50 (*to* ALBERTINE AT 70). You're not alone. Think of us. We're all here, with you . . .

ALBERTINE AT 70. Not all of you are a consolation . . .

ALBERTINE AT 50. Don't just think of our bad points . . . There are times . . . times when you were okay . . . Look at Thérèse and Marcel . . . We know what became of them, and it's easy to dwell on that . . . but how about when they were little, eh? Did you ever see two such adorable babies? You remember?

ALBERTINE AT 70. Yes, I remember, but it's no comfort . . .

ALBERTINE AT 50. Try . . . for my sake.

ALBERTINE AT 70. Mind you, they were lovely babies. When Thérèse was small, people would stop me on the street to tell me how lovely she was . . .

ALBERTINE AT 50. And Marcel . . .

ALBERTINE AT 70. Marcel had too much imagination . . . he frightened me, even when he was little . . .

ALBERTINE AT 50. But think of all the cuddles . . . how he'd laugh when he was happy . . .

ALBERTINE AT 70. None of that's clear for me now . . . What became of them is too painful . . . I can't recall the good moments . . . I'm sorry.

ALBERTINE AT 60. Impotence . . .

ALBERTINE AT 50. If it's not clear . . . make it up. If the past is too painful, invent a new one . . . Do what I did, forget! At least try. You'll see, it's not so hard. When a bad memory tries to get me, I shake it off . . . If I'm in the house, I get out . . . If I'm at work, I sing . . . I turn my back on it, leave it behind.

ALBERTINE AT 70. Where can I go? Out in the hall? They'd catch up with me in no time. You see, I can't go anywhere, I can't rebel.

ALBERTINE AT 60. Exactly. That's why I'm resigned to it. You can never get away, never!

ALBERTINE AT 70. You're not resigned to anything. You've just let go. You've given up . . . life. It's not the same.

ALBERTINE AT 50. That's right . . . so don't copy her.

ALBERTINE AT 60. You talk about me like I'm dead.

ALBERTINE AT 70 *looks at her, then turns away.*

ALBERTINE AT 70 (*to* ALBERTINE AT 50, *tapping her on the hand*). I'll be okay . . .

ALBERTINE AT 50 *slowly leaves her.*

ALBERTINE AT 40. It's like a ball of fire, Madeleine . . .

ALBERTINE AT 30. Yes . . . A ball of fire in my chest . . .

ALBERTINE AT 40. . . . . that never stops burning.

ALBERTINE AT 30. Even if I scream, if I hit people, it's still there . . . even after I've calmed down . . .

ALBERTINE AT 40. Sometimes it hurts so much I can't do a thing . . . I have to lie down on the bed . . . but then it gets worse . . .

ALBERTINE AT 30. To lie on your bed in a rage, Madeleine . . . is horrible!

MADELEINE. But what gets you so enraged?

ALBERTINE AT 40. Everything!

ALBERTINE AT 30. That's right, I take everything badly . . . Even the good times . . . the few I get. When something goes right for me I don't trust it . . . I think there's something dreadful I can't see, and it's going to pounce on me.

MADELEINE. Why not enjoy the good times while they're happening . . .

ALBERTINE AT 30. I can't.

ALBERTINE AT 50. That's not true . . .

ALBERTINE AT 40. They're always followed by something hideous. (*To* ALBERTINE AT 50.) You'll see!

MADELEINE. But what happens to everyone. We're all the same. You don't have a monopoly on suffering.

ALBERTINE AT 40. Will you stop telling me that! I know I don't have a monopoly on suffering. But how come what happens to me is always worse than what happens to others?

MADELEINE. Because you make it worse. Instead of looking for a solution, you rush headlong into tragedy and disaster.

ALBERTINE AT 30. Easy for you to say, nothing ever happens to you.

MADELEINE. You think that because I don't complain, Bartine. I keep my troubles to myself. Deal with them myself.

ALBERTINE AT 60. I do that now too, Madeleine . . . I took your advice . . . I stay quiet in my room, I don't bother a soul . . .

She opens a small bottle of pills and takes one with a glass of water.

And for the first time, I've got peace.

ALBERTINE AT 50. You've got a short memory.

ALBERTINE AT 60. What? I don't know what you mean.

ALBERTINE AT 50. I've stopped complaining too . . . But I don't take pills . . .

ALBERTINE AT 60. That won't last . . .

ALBERTINE AT 50. Why shouldn't it?

ALBERTINE AT 60. Because you're play-acting. You're going through a phase where you play at being happy and positive.

ALBERTINE AT 70. Oh, shut up!

ALBERTINE AT 60. You're no different! You've convinced yourself you'll be happy in your stinky little room, but the real you knows better.

ALBERTINE AT 70. At least I'm glad to be alive . . .

ALBERTINE AT 50. So am I . . . glad to be alive . . .

ALBERTINE AT 60. I don't believe you.

ALBERTINE AT 30. I'm young, I'm strong, I could do so much if it weren't for this rage, gnawing at me . . .

ALBERTINE AT 40. Sometimes I think it's all that keeps me alive . . .

ALBERTINE AT 30. It's true . . .

ALBERTINE AT 60. You'll get over that, too . . . Rage . . . Rebellion never solved a thing.

ALBERTINE AT 30. I'll tell you why I'm here this week, Madeleine, you'll understand . . . You'll understand what I mean by this rage.

Silence. The other ALBERTINES *and* MADELEINE *listen carefully.*

My child, my own daughter, my Thérèse, who I fight with all

the time because we're so alike . . . though I try to bring her up as best I can . . . It's true, you know, I do the best I can . . . I don't know much, but what I do know I try to pass on to my kids . . . though they never listen. Another thing that enrages me . . . Anyway . . . my Thérèse who I always thought was so innocent, with her dolls and those girlfriends she leads around by the nose . . . Believe it or not, she was seeing a man. A man, Madeleine, not some brat her own age who'd be happy to kiss her with her mouth closed, but a grown man!

MADELEINE. Are you sure? She's only eleven!

ALBERTINE AT 30. When I found out I went berserk . . . I mean, you'd have done the same. I know, don't say it, your daughter would never do that . . .

MADELEINE. But who is he? Did you ever see them together?

ALBERTINE AT 30. Of course not, for God's sake, I'd have murdered him long ago! She wasn't seeing him . . . actually going out with him, no, that's not what I mean . . .

Silence.

ALBERTINE AT 70. Go on . . . it'll do you good.

ALBERTINE AT 30. I know it will, but I can't. (*She takes two or three deep breaths.*) Did you ever want to destroy everything around you? Did you ever feel you had the strength to destroy everything? (*She searches for the words.*) Men . . . men . . . men . . . They're the ones, Madeleine. They're the ones. Not us.

MADELEINE *approaches her sister and takes her in her arms.* ALBERTINE AT 30 *withdraws from this timid hug.*

Eleven years old, Madeleine, and he was chasing her like she was a woman! Following her everywhere. And she let him do what he liked, without a word. She knew, and she didn't say a word!

ALBERTINE AT 40. She liked it.

ALBERTINE AT 30. She liked it, Madeleine, she told me herself. And that's why I beat her.

ALBERTINE AT 40. And she still likes it . . . after all that's happened . . . that's what's killing me.

ALBERTINE AT 50. Why drag it all up again? Leave it be, for God's sake!

ALBERTINE AT 30. Naturally I found out by accident. I was lying on the sofa the other day, in the middle of the afternoon . . . I could feel a storm brewing . . . Mother'd been in a rotten mood all day, the kids were driving me nuts . . . Thérèse came to sit on the front balcony with her friend Pierrette.

Silence.

ALBERTINE AT 40. They talked about it like it was an everyday thing . . .

ALL FIVE ALBERTINES (*in alternation*). Pierrette asked Thérèse if she'd seen her 'gent' lately and she said he disappeared the beginning of June. I assumed it was some neighbourhood kid, and I figured: 'Here we go, boy problems. Already.' Then I realized it wasn't that at all. They were talking about him like he was an actor, for God's sake. Comparing him to those movie stars in the magazines . . . They even said he was better looking! I lay there, horrified . . . They had no idea . . . of the danger . . . the danger of men, Madeleine . . .

ALBERTINE AT 30. And when Thérèse started talking about the last time she saw him, how he got down on his knees in front of her right on the street and put his head on . . . her belly, I got up, not knowing what I was doing and went out on the balcony . . .

ALL FIVE ALBERTINES (*in alternation*). . . . and I started to hit her, Madeleine.

ALBERTINE AT 30. I didn't know where I was hitting. I just hit her as hard as I could. Thérèse was screaming, Pierrette was crying, the neighbours coming out of their houses . . . and I didn't stop . . . I couldn't. It wasn't just Thérèse I was hitting, it was . . . my whole life . . . I couldn't find the words to explain the danger, so I just hit! (*She turns toward her sister.*) I never told Thérèse much about men 'cause the words would have been filthy. (*Silence.*) If Gabriel hadn't come out and separated us, I would have killed her.

MADELEINE *puts her hand on her sister's shoulder who throws herself into her arms.*

I didn't cry, Madeleine. Not once. And I still can't. (*Silence.*) Rage.

ALBERTINE AT 40. Thérèse was never worth tears.

ALBERTINE AT 70. How can you say that? She's your child!

ALBERTINE AT 40. And yours. Do you even remember her? Shed tears for her?

Silence.

ALBERTINE AT 70. I have my regrets.

ALBERTINE AT 40. But no tears.

Silence.

ALBERTINE AT 70. I never knew how to cry.

ALBERTINE AT 30 *and* MADELEINE *have sat down on the steps.*

ALBERTINE AT 30. Is that what the doctor said in his letter?

MADELEINE. No. He said you gave Thérèse a beating. Since neither of you told him why, he didn't know.

ALBERTINE AT 30. I guess he thinks I'm crazier than ever.

MADELEINE. No one thinks you're crazy.

ALBERTINE AT 30. But I am, you know. When your child's in danger and you beat her instead of explaining it to her, isn't that crazy?

ALBERTINE AT 70. No, it's not crazy. It's ignorance.

MADELEINE *lowers her eyes.*

ALBERTINE AT 70 (*to* MADELEINE). Why don't you tell her?

MADELEINE. What . . .

ALBERTINE AT 70. That it's ignorance . . .

MADELEINE. You don't just tell your sister she's ignorant.

ALBERTINE AT 70. If it can help her . . .

MADELEINE. And what if it doesn't?

ALBERTINE AT 70. Well I'll tell you, you're ignorant, even if you are my sister.

MADELEINE. I see you haven't changed as much as I thought.

ALBERTINE AT 70. Don't misunderstand. If you tell her she's not crazy, she'll believe you; if you tell her it's ignorance, and ignorance can be overcome, that may encourage her . . . I don't know . . . to find out, ask questions . . .

ALBERTINE AT 30. Never mind . . . don't bother. It's nice that you care, but whether I'm stupid or crazy won't change a thing. I know I'm not like the others . . .

ALBERTINE AT 70 (*gently*). But . . . the others are no smarter.

ALBERTINE AT 40. That's why I yell at them, too!

ALBERTINE AT 70. Excuse me, I'm not talking to you . . . (*To* ALBERTINE AT 30.) We all depend on you . . .
Try . . . to talk to Thérèse . . . to understand Marcel. Once they're gone, it will be too late . . .

ALBERTINE AT 50. Not for me . . .

ALBERTINE AT 30. I try sometimes . . . I really do. But we're the same, all three of us . . . pigheaded . . . and . . . we can't talk to one another. (*To* ALBERTINE AT 70.) Don't judge me. You've forgotten how hard it is.

ALBERTINE AT 70. Mind you . . . there's no point in asking people to change . . . When you're young you think you're right . . . when you get older you realize you were wrong . . . what's the point of it all? We should have the right to a second life . . . but we're so badly made . . . I doubt we'd do any better.

ALBERTINE AT 30 (*to* MADELEINE). Did the doctor ask you to try and get me to talk?

MADELEINE. No.

Silence.

ALBERTINE AT 30. What am I going to do, Madeleine?

MADELEINE. Do you know who the guy is?

ALBERTINE AT 30. I think he works at parc Lafontaine. They're the worst. They're supposed to keep an eye on our kids, and they spend their time ogling them . . . I'll sick the cops on him when I get home . . .

ALBERTINE AT 40. No, you won't sick the cops on him . . . All you'll do is punish Thérèse and try to forget. And when you do find him, it'll be too late.

ALBERTINE AT 30. But that's not what I meant . . . What do I do for the rest of my life? If I beat my kids just 'cause I can't talk to them, does that mean they'll lock me up? Even when I'm right?

ALBERTINE AT 60. No, they won't do that . . . You'll lock them
up . . .

ALBERTINE AT 30. Me, lock up my kids? What do you mean?

ALBERTINE AT 50. Never mind, I know what she's up
to . . .

ALBERTINE AT 60. You're scared, huh?

ALBERTINE AT 50. Yes. I'm scared of your version.

ALBERTINE AT 60. There's more than one?

ALBERTINE AT 50. Okay, if we really have to talk about it, let
me go first . . . then we'll see.

ALBERTINE AT 60. Don't listen to her. She'll embellish it, she'll
make herself look good.

ALBERTINE AT 50. I'll tell what happened, the way it happened.

Silence.

ALBERTINE AT 70. Be careful . . . this is a delicate
matter . . .

ALBERTINE AT 50. I know, but I'm not ashamed of it.

ALBERTINE AT 70. Fine. Go ahead . . .

ALBERTINE AT 50. One day I discovered something really
important. I did it myself, too, even if I'm no genius . . . I was
thinking about my kids and my family who never listened to
me, never gave me the time of time, never asked my opinion
and who treated me like I didn't exist. And I discovered that to
make yourself heard in this life, you have to *disobey*. If you
really want something, you *disobey*. Otherwise you get crushed. I
always listened to others, took their advice, did what they
wanted, you, Madeleine, our two brothers, mother . . . but at
the age of fifty I disobeyed, and I'm not sorry.

ALBERTINE AT 60. You will be . . .

ALBERTINE AT 50. It was hard at first . . . I'd always depended
totally on others. No kidding, if someone didn't tell me what to
do, I asked. I begged! I spent my life begging. There I was,
stuck in this houseful of people, and I couldn't budge until
someone said it was okay. And all that did was feed my rage . . . I
was always about to explode. But at the age of fifty I thought,
don't ask me any more. Disobey. Try it, just once. Find out if it

works. But I had this huge weight holding me back . . . Marcel.
Thérèse had disappeared long ago. I never heard from her
except when they found her drunk in some alley, or she'd
phone me from headquarters 'cause they'd just picked her up . . .
How many times I had to scrape together the twenty-five bucks,
then take the Saint-Denis bus . . . I tell this like it was nothing,
but . . . we get numbed by the pain, I guess . . . So Marcel was
all I had left, twenty-five years old, barely responsible, a child
for life, who I was still protecting and would go on protecting
until one of us dropped because I never could understand
him . . . He withdrew more and more, drifted away from me,
yet still demanding I be there . . . I watched him . . . Yes, I
watched him go mad . . . I'm sorry, this isn't easy . . .

ALBERTINE AT 60. Costs a lot to disobey, huh?

ALBERTINE AT 70 (*to* ALBERTINE AT 60). Will you please shut
up!

ALBERTINE AT 50 (*to* MADELEINE). I didn't stick to my role,
Madeleine, I disobeyed. I know what you all thought, but you
were wrong. If I hadn't done it, if I were still the prisoner of a
madman, a madman who had me in the palm of his hand, who
was growing more and more dangerous . . . that's not a role for
anyone. I broke the mould, I stopped being mother hen.
(*Silence*.) I told Thérèse I'd have nothing more to do with her . . .
and I had Marcel put away, far from here . . .

MADELEINE *turns away*.

It hurt, but you want to know the truth? I've never been
happier in my life, and neither have they. They're with their
own kind, and so am I.

ALBERTINE AT 40. You should have done it sooner . . . If I had
the guts . . . but I'm scared what people would think.
(*Ironically*.) We play our roles to the bitter end, don't we? So
they always told us. You brought a crazy kid into the world, it's
your fault, pay!

ALBERTINE AT 50. When it was over, and I'd done it, and I
found myself alone, it was incredible. A feeling I'd never
known. My days were mine, no one to worry about . . . I
bought new clothes, not expensive, but nice, and I went out to
find a job. Do you realize what that means? A job. Freedom!

ALBERTINE AT 70. My first job. My only job. Le parc
Lafontaine.

ALBERTINE AT 50. The only park I've ever known, the only bit of green, and it's mine. I work in the restaurant at parc Lafontaine, right in the very heart where everyone goes . . . and they say I make the best bacon, lettuce and tomato sandwich with mayo in the world! People come here especially for my BLT's. They come to me 'cause I'm the best! And what's more, I get paid! The customers and the other employees love me, and they treat me like a queen because I feed them like they used to get fed at home.

ALBERTINE AT 60. You wait on people like you always did.

ALBERTINE AT 50. At least I'm not down on all fours cleaning up Marcel's mess or getting ulcers 'cause Thérèse has pulled another stunt! I come here singing in the morning, I sing while I work, and I go home singing at night. I watch the sun set in summer and the kids skating in winter. I earn my living, do you understand? I live as I please without family on my back, without kids, without men! Oh yes, no men. By choice. And I'm happy. I held myself back too long, Madeleine. I had to disobey!

MADELEINE. You hate them that much?

ALBERTINE AT 30. My kids?

ALBERTINE AT 50. I love my kids more than my life, Madeleine. But they're better off away from me, and I'm better off away from them.

MADELEINE. I'm not talking to you . . . (*To* ALBERTINE AT 30.) I don't mean your kids . . .

ALBERTINE AT 50. You've had enough of me?

MADELEINE. I'm talking about men.

ALBERTINE AT 30 *stiffens. She doesn't answer.*

ALBERTINE AT 60. Who wants to listen to a heartless cow?

ALBERTINE AT 70. Why heartless?

ALBERTINE AT 60. To abandon her kids . . .

ALBERTINE AT 40. I understand you.

ALBERTINE AT 70. So do I . . . I think.

MADELEINE. Because you knew one who was a bastard doesn't mean they're all like that.

Silence. ALBERTINE AT 50 *laughs wickedly.*

ALBERTINE AT 50. The gospel according to Madeleine! I know it by heart.

MADELEINE. Soon, in about half an hour . . . we're going to see two lights in the distance . . . two narrow beams that will light up the pines on either side of the highway . . . The car will turn left up the driveway . . . Alex will be home . . . with treats for me and the kids . . . corn on the cob, though it's not in season yet, or candies, or a nice plump chicken he's got in exchange for God knows what . . . You know salesmen, all kinds of tricks up their sleeves . . . He'll give me a little wave as he gets out of the car. I'll go down the steps to meet him . . . It's exciting, a kiss in the dark. His eyes will be gentle when he looks at me, even though he can't see me, and I can't see him either.

ALBERTINE AT 50. Her favourite role . . . always the same . . .

ALBERTINE AT 70. You were so naive, Madeleine . . .

MADELEINE. Alex is a good man, Bartine . . .

ALBERTINE AT 30. Well, that's fine for you . . . but he's the only one you've ever known.

MADELEINE. I prefer to think well of them.

ALBERTINE AT 30. Well, I don't. Wait till your daughter comes to you with a problem like Thérèse's . . .

MADELEINE. That's not likely. My daughter and I talk . . .

ALBERTINE AT 40. Talk to Thérèse, see how much fun that is! You can't, I've been telling you for ten years. She's not a little girl any more, she's got real problems!

MADELEINE. You don't know how to deal with her . . .

ALBERTINE AT 40. I've tried everything under the sun! All she does is shit on me, then goes right back to her pimps and whores.

ALBERTINE AT 30. I don't want her to end up like me, but I don't want her to rebel so much she ruins her life.

ALBERTINE AT 40. Well, that's what she's done. And it's no fun to watch.

ALBERTINE AT 30. I wish I knew what to tell her.

ALBERTINE AT 40. Don't worry. She'll choose for herself . . . All
you can do is watch her go and have a good cry, 'cause you're
going to feel responsible. It's always our fault. Always!

ALBERTINE AT 30. Before you know it she'll be a woman,
cooped up like the rest of us. Or cast out like the lepers . . .
Did it ever strike you, Madeleine, with all your brains, that
those are our only choices?

MADELEINE. Would you be any happier if you'd made the
other one?

ALBERTINE AT 30. That's not the point. If I were younger, I'd
look for a third choice . . . (*Silence*.) That's what I'll tell
Thérèse . . . If I can ever talk to her . . .

MADELEINE. No harm trying.

ALBERTINE AT 40. I did try. (*To* ALBERTINE AT 50.) You did
the right thing.

ALBERTINE AT 30 (*to* MADELEINE). What do you think of
that?

MADELEINE. If my daughter does what I've done, I don't think
she'll be wrong.

ALBERTINE AT 70. Poor Madeleine. But maybe you were right.
Maybe there's more than one truth. Sometimes what's true for
us doesn't hold for someone else. You were happy the way you
were, Madeleine. When you come right down to it, I was
probably jealous . . .

ALBERTINE AT 30. I'm not jealous of her!

ALBERTINE AT 40. Me neither!

ALBERTINE AT 70. You just never admitted it . . .

ALBERTINE AT 50. At times . . . I don't mean I'm jealous
exactly, no, no, I like my independence too much . . . But
when she comes to see me at the restaurant, with her little
granddaughter, all dressed up, I think maybe I'd have liked
that too, grandchildren to play with, and
spoil . . .

ALBERTINE AT 70. Mind you, if I hadn't married a buffoon, I
might have felt differently.

ALBERTINE AT 40. Oh, come off it! She's right, men are all the

same, they get us every time. They're in control, what do you
expect? As long as we let them, they take advantage. 'Cause
they're not idiots. It's their world, they made it. Thérèse got a
taste of that, you know. Prince Charming on a fake charger with
a rented costume! Believe it or not, she came home one day
with a guy who looked normal. Like a jerk, I figured leave well
enough alone, he's better than what she usually drags in! You
can't imagine the winners I've seen, things the lowest whore
wouldn't touch! Anyway . . . he was good looking, he was nice,
he had gentle eyes. Halleluia! But when I asked him what he
did for a living and he told me he was a bus driver, I figured
this is too good . . . something's fishy . . . And wouldn't you
know it, he told me he'd known Thérèse for a long time. Ten
years ago he was an attendant at parc Lafontaine . . .

ALBERTINE AT 30 *starts.*

Oh yes . . . It all fit, he was about ten years older than her, it
all made sense . . . It took him ten years to get her, and he got
her. And Thérèse knows the score. She's not eleven any more,
she's twenty, she knows what she's doing. And she knows what
he wanted to do to her. But here's what infuriates me . . . she's
decided she's going to marry him! 'Cause he's handsome.
'Cause other women are jealous. 'Cause it pisses me off! And
you wonder why I want to kill! My own daughter's going to
marry a man who almost raped her ten years ago . . . who
could start again at any time with anybody. That's it, that's men
in a nutshell: they find a hole, they stick it in!

Long embarrassed silence.

ALBERTINE AT 40. Forgive me. You especially, Madeleine. What
you don't know won't hurt you, but I'll bet your Alex isn't
perfect. It's not possible. He's got to be hiding something.

ALBERTINE AT 70. He's not expected to be perfect. Watch
out . . . you're making judgements . . .

ALBERTINE AT 60. And I suppose you don't? You won't look at
me, won't speak to me . . . you act like I don't exist!

ALBERTINE AT 70. I'm not perfect either . . .

ALBERTINE AT 40. Anyway, her Alex . . . I never trusted him.

ALBERTINE AT 50. That's not true . . . In fact you had your eye
on him once . . .

ALBERTINE AT 40. That twerp? Come off it!

ALBERTINE AT 70. But it's true. I remember. He was a twerp, but that was his charm . . . You could tell he wasn't dangerous . . . But Madeleine was too fast for me . . .

MADELEINE. Stop talking about me like I'm not here! And don't talk about Alex that way, it's embarrassing . . .

ALBERTINE AT 50. No one will steal your prince . . .

ALBERTINE AT 40. God, no!

MADELEINE. If you don't want to believe me, don't . . . I'm sure you have your reasons for hating men . . . (*She smiles*.) I don't . . . Maybe I'm content with very little, maybe my happiness is trite and insignificant, but . . . (*Silence*.) It's funny . . . I don't care. I think . . . I think I'd rather be happy in my own modest way than spend my life living some grand tragedy. (*Silence*.) When those two beams of light come round the bend, you can all rest assured, I'll be happy, perfectly happy . . . and that's all I have to say.

ALBERTINE AT 70 (*softly*). You've been gone so long, Madeleine, I have trouble seeing you clearly. I remember you well but the image is blurred . . . I know you were a good person . . . the best in the family. Mind you, Gabriel and Edouard were okay, but they were men . . . You were always so patient . . .

MADELEINE. You talk about me in the past. That means I'm not here, doesn't it?

ALBERTINE AT 70. Yes. You've been gone . . . oh . . . I was still working at parc Lafontaine . . . That's a good twenty years . . .

MADELEINE. I won't have lived long . . . Was I happy till the end?

ALBERTINE AT 70. Come over here and sit beside me . . .

MADELEINE *sits at her sister's feet.*

I thought your hair was redder.

MADELEINE. Red?

ALBERTINE AT 70. As I recall, your hair was red that summer . . .

MADELEINE. It was the sun . . .

ALBERTINE AT 30. If I spent three years in the sun, my hair would still be black.

ALBERTINE AT 70. When you left us, I lost my only confidante . . . The phone didn't ring any more . . . Ah! For a long time we didn't talk much 'cause you were mad when I turned my back on the kids . . . though deep down, I think you understood . . . but we started phoning again, at first just to keep in touch, then 'cause we really needed to see each other . . . and when you brought your granddaughter to see me for the first time, and I saw how fat you'd gotten . . . I laughed so hard! Mind you, maybe that's why I have trouble remembering you . . . The last few times I saw you, you were so fat . . .

MADELEINE. Don't exaggerate!

ALBERTINE AT 70. Well . . .

ALBERTINE AT 50. We didn't recognize each other. I missed you so much!

Silence.

MADELEINE. Bartine . . . Did I suffer much before I died?

ALBERTINE AT 70 (*after hesitating*). Yes . . . Don't go . . . stay with me a bit . . . The night will be long . . .

MADELEINE. You're right, it does smell funny here . . .

ALBERTINE AT 70. You see, I don't notice it any more . . . I've already forgotten . . .

ALBERTINE AT 30. It's getting chilly, eh?

MADELEINE. You're not used to it. It's August, summer's nearly over. But wait and see how well you'll sleep!

ALBERTINE AT 70. I hope so . . .

MADELEINE. You want a sweater?

ALBERTINE AT 30. No, no . . .

ALBERTINE AT 40. Hasn't been so cold this early for a long time . . . Another rotten summer!

ALBERTINE AT 30. I want to wait for your Prince Charming with his light beams.

They smile at each other.

I'd like to be far away from the house right now . . . Maybe on top of that mountain . . . From up there, the house must look tiny . . . Close your eyes, try to imagine that's where we are . . .

Can you see it, way down below? A flicker of light, shining on the edge of night . . . It looks so peaceful from a distance. Two women on a verandah. I wonder what they're talking about. They look so happy. Both of them.

Silence.

Do you think they look happy?

MADELEINE. Yes.

ALBERTINE AT 30. Shall we visit them? Maybe they can tell us their secret . . . You know it already but I . . .

ALBERTINE AT 40. It's so dark. Why haven't they turned on the streetlights?

ALBERTINE AT 50. It's dark because the moon's not up yet. I like that. I feel protected.

ALBERTINE AT 30. Normally I'm scared of the dark, but here it's inviting . . . In the city I'm never aware the world exists, so vast . . . overwhelming. (*Silence.*) In the city, the world seems small.

ALBERTINE AT 40. I suffocate in the dark . . . like the world's closing in on me.

ALBERTINE AT 30. In the city, the world doesn't exist.

ALBERTINE AT 50. When I was a kid, sometimes I'd imagine there was nothing beyond my school . . . My school was the world. A world with only kids. Little girls, skipping.

ALBERTINE AT 30. Here goes . . . I'm going to cry. No. Not yet. God, that's what I need, a really good cry!

ALBERTINE AT 40. I try sometimes. In bed. I go deep down inside myself, I tell myself you've got to cry, it'll do you good. But it's no use. I have no reason to cry, just to scream. When Thérèse shows up in the morning, bruised, drunk, trying to butter me up because she feels guilty, but still being a smart-ass 'cause it's the only way she can show her independence, how can I cry? I scream! She screams back, I scream louder, then mother joins in . . . If the three of us stood face to face, screaming our heads off, it would have precisely the same effect. We don't listen to what anyone's saying, we listen to ourselves scream! Thérèse is down at the French Casino on la rue Saint-Laurent surrounded by drunks, whores and drug addicts. That's her problem. I've raised two kids for nothing and I feel guilty because I know I did it badly. That's my problem. Mother had to leave her house at Duhamel to come and live in the city, and she's never got over it. That's her problem. Three brilliant generations!

ALBERTINE AT 70. And instead of trying to understand, you do nothing but insult each other . . .

ALBERTINE AT 40 *looks at her.*

ALBERTINE AT 40. I have enough problems, I don't need other people's!

ALBERTINE AT 70. That's why you'll never get anywhere.

ALBERTINE AT 50 (*to* ALBERTINE AT 40). And you want us to believe you're intelligent!

ALBERTINE AT 40. But I can't solve them. I've never set foot on la rue Saint-Laurent, it terrifies me, and I've spent one week of my life at Duhamel.

ALBERTINE AT 50. That has nothing to do with it! Besides, they don't expect you to solve their problems, they only ask you to listen.

ALBERTINE AT 40. They don't listen to me, why should I listen to them?

ALBERTINE AT 50 *and* 70 *sigh in exasperation.*

ALBERTINE AT 50. There's no point trying to talk to you, is there?

MADELEINE *gets up and goes toward* ALBERTINE AT 50.

MADELEINE. How did you find out . . . I was gone?

ALBERTINE AT 50. The telephone rang here one night. I had my coat on, I was about to leave . . .

MADELEINE. It must have been a shock . . .

ALBERTINE AT 50. No . . . We'd been expecting it. You were sick for a long time, you know . . .

MADELEINE. I don't want to hear any more.

She runs back to the Duhamel house, taking refuge with ALBERTINE AT 30.

I'm glad! You never know, the door I
place bearable. It can't be worse than

around her.

you, you're right, it's not as bad. They're
toxicate you, put you into a new 'home'
are you of everything, except your

to be late . . . That's what happens when
going in, it's cold . . .

ay for a bit . . .

sweater?

. . Look, goosebumps . . .

morrow . . .

morrow . . .

the road). If he gets home before you go
ake any noise. If I'm asleep he won't
awake, I'll let him know one way or

eine . . .

worry about it . . . getting old's not

res to go into the house. ALBERTINE AT 50
difficulty, ALBERTINE AT 60 *opens her*
INE AT 70 *sighs.*

one in the middle of the world.

anything to keep that from happening!

luck . . .

Thérèse would come home . . . Please,
ng crazy tonight . . .

ALBERTINE AT 50. I didn't go home. I went straight to your place to be with Alex . . .

ALBERTINE AT 30. Is that him? Look, I see headlights on the road . . .

MADELEINE. No, they're too big . . . must be a truck.

ALBERTINE AT 50. But . . . Alex was inconsolable.

ALBERTINE AT 40. All the while, Marcel creeps around, watching us . . . He doesn't cry when we fight, he laughs. A maddening, nervous laugh. In his crazy eyes there's this . . . pleading look . . . as if he were saying: 'don't fight, it makes me laugh, I'm so frightened, you'll make me laugh!' (*Silence. She screams.*) If I'd strangled them both when I saw they weren't normal, I wouldn't be saddled with all this now!

ALBERTINE AT 60. More guilt . . .

ALBERTINE AT 40. Sure, it was drilled into us, what do you expect?

ALBERTINE AT 70 (*to* ALBERTINE AT 60). What can you feel guilty about, you're drugged to the eyeballs?

ALBERTINE AT 60. So, you've finally noticed I'm here!

ALBERTINE AT 70. How can I help it, you stick your nose in everything.

ALBERTINE AT 60. Don't I have a right to speak? Are you ashamed?

ALBERTINE AT 70. Yes.

ALBERTINE AT 60. Mind you, you're probably right . . . So be ashamed, and leave me alone . . .

ALBERTINE AT 70. I asked you a question . . .

ALBERTINE AT 60. Don't pretend you don't know the answer. You can't have forgotten, I'm not that far behind you.

ALBERTINE AT 70. I want to hear you say it out loud . . .

ALBERTINE AT 60. Why, if you remember?

ALBERTINE AT 70. To make sure . . . my memories are as terrible as I think . . . so I can start selecting again . . .

ALBERTINE AT 60. It's true, I've never told anyone . . . I kept it

to myself . . . Look . . . my hands are shaking . . . my mouth's
dry . . . but I can't take another yet, I have to wait half an
hour . . . or it'll make me sick instead of better . . . Once . . .
when the pain was unbearable . . . I took three . . . just to see . . .
I ended up on the floor beside the bed . . . I was unconscious
for hours . . . But if you only knew how good it feels . . . when
I don't overdo it. They're wonderful, these things, you know.
They . . . lighten you is how the doctor described it . . .
I don't feel that knot in my throat, the weight on my heart . . .
I can breathe freely . . . It vibrates around me, as if I can hear
the motor of things . . . It's true . . . sometimes I lie on my bed
and I listen to the motor of things . . . The world is a huge
clock . . . everything has its purpose . . .

ALBERTINE AT 40. Even you?

ALBERTINE AT 60 (*looking at* ALBERTINE AT 50). Mine is to
pay for those who have no heart. I fooled myself for a while. I
thought things would be okay . . . I went my own way, thinking
the rest of the world wouldn't follow . . . but it did.

ALBERTINE AT 50. No!

ALBERTINE AT 60. Oh yes, it followed!

ALBERTINE AT 50. I don't believe you!

ALBERTINE AT 60. You can't afford to . . . Hang on to your
illusions as long as you can . . . gain time, it's running out
fast . . .

ALBERTINE AT 40. What made you fall so low? What happened?

ALBERTINE AT 60 (*to* ALBERTINE AT 70). Now do you
remember?

ALBERTINE AT 70. Of course . . . I never forgot . . .

ALBERTINE AT 60. One morning the police knocked on the door
. . . I was getting ready to go to work . . . I was singing . . . Right
away I knew something had happened to Thérèse. The two cops
sat down in the living room. I looked at their long faces and I
thought: Any minute now the world's going to come crashing
down on my shoulders. And the world came crashing down on
my shoulders . . .

Silence.

(*Very gently.*) They told me they'd found Thérèse in a room on
Saint-Laurent. They weren't sure if she'd died of natural causes or

ALBERTINE AT 60. Good
open may lead to some
here!

ALBERTINE AT 70 *look*

ALBERTINE AT 70. Mind
going to revive you, dei
as they say . . . They'll
memories . . .

MADELEINE. He's going
he travels too far . . . I'

ALBERTINE AT 30. I'll st

MADELEINE. You want a

ALBERTINE AT 30. Yes .

MADELEINE. We'll talk t

ALBERTINE AT 30. Yes,

MADELEINE (*looking out*
to bed, tell him not to
wake me . . . and if I'm
another . . .

ALBERTINE AT 70. Mad

MADELEINE. Yes . . .

ALBERTINE AT 70. Don'
worth it . . .

MADELEINE *goes out.*

Silence.

ALBERTINE AT 40 *prep*
wipes her counter top. With
container of pills. ALBERT

ALBERTINE AT 30. All a

ALBERTINE AT 50. I'll d
Anything!

ALBERTINE AT 60. Good

ALBERTINE AT 40. If on
don't let her do somethi

ALBERTINE AT 50. I didn't go home. I went straight to your place to be with Alex . . .

ALBERTINE AT 30. Is that him? Look, I see headlights on the road . . .

MADELEINE. No, they're too big . . . must be a truck.

ALBERTINE AT 50. But . . . Alex was inconsolable.

ALBERTINE AT 40. All the while, Marcel creeps around, watching us . . . He doesn't cry when we fight, he laughs. A maddening, nervous laugh. In his crazy eyes there's this . . . pleading look . . . as if he were saying: 'don't fight, it makes me laugh, I'm so frightened, you'll make me laugh!' (*Silence. She screams.*) If I'd strangled them both when I saw they weren't normal, I wouldn't be saddled with all this now!

ALBERTINE AT 60. More guilt . . .

ALBERTINE AT 40. Sure, it was drilled into us, what do you expect?

ALBERTINE AT 70 (*to* ALBERTINE AT 60). What can you feel guilty about, you're drugged to the eyeballs?

ALBERTINE AT 60. So, you've finally noticed I'm here!

ALBERTINE AT 70. How can I help it, you stick your nose in everything.

ALBERTINE AT 60. Don't I have a right to speak? Are you ashamed?

ALBERTINE AT 70. Yes.

ALBERTINE AT 60. Mind you, you're probably right . . . So be ashamed, and leave me alone . . .

ALBERTINE AT 70. I asked you a question . . .

ALBERTINE AT 60. Don't pretend you don't know the answer. You can't have forgotten, I'm not that far behind you.

ALBERTINE AT 70. I want to hear you say it out loud . . .

ALBERTINE AT 60. Why, if you remember?

ALBERTINE AT 70. To make sure . . . my memories are as terrible as I think . . . so I can start selecting again . . .

ALBERTINE AT 60. It's true, I've never told anyone . . . I kept it

to myself . . . Look . . . my hands are shaking . . . my mouth's
dry . . . but I can't take another yet, I have to wait half an
hour . . . or it'll make me sick instead of better . . . Once . . .
when the pain was unbearable . . . I took three . . . just to see . . .
I ended up on the floor beside the bed . . . I was unconscious
for hours . . . But if you only knew how good it feels . . . when
I don't overdo it. They're wonderful, these things, you know.
They . . . lighten you is how the doctor described it . . .
I don't feel that knot in my throat, the weight on my heart . . .
I can breathe freely . . . It vibrates around me, as if I can hear
the motor of things . . . It's true . . . sometimes I lie on my bed
and I listen to the motor of things . . . The world is a huge
clock . . . everything has its purpose . . .

ALBERTINE AT 40. Even you?

ALBERTINE AT 60 (*looking at* ALBERTINE AT 50). Mine is to
pay for those who have no heart. I fooled myself for a while. I
thought things would be okay . . . I went my own way, thinking
the rest of the world wouldn't follow . . . but it did.

ALBERTINE AT 50. No!

ALBERTINE AT 60. Oh yes, it followed!

ALBERTINE AT 50. I don't believe you!

ALBERTINE AT 60. You can't afford to . . . Hang on to your
illusions as long as you can . . . gain time, it's running out
fast . . .

ALBERTINE AT 40. What made you fall so low? What happened?

ALBERTINE AT 60 (*to* ALBERTINE AT 70). Now do you
remember?

ALBERTINE AT 70. Of course . . . I never forgot . . .

ALBERTINE AT 60. One morning the police knocked on the door
. . . I was getting ready to go to work . . . I was singing . . . Right
away I knew something had happened to Thérèse. The two cops
sat down in the living room. I looked at their long faces and I
thought: Any minute now the world's going to come crashing
down on my shoulders. And the world came crashing down on
my shoulders . . .

Silence.

(*Very gently.*) They told me they'd found Thérèse in a room on
Saint-Laurent. They weren't sure if she'd died of natural causes or

if someone had . . . she was soaked in her own blood . . . I had to go and identify the body, I was the closest relative. The closest relative . . . I made her for God's sake! And her husband, ha! He'd disappeared long ago, I always knew he would. So, with the world on my shoulders, I went to identify the body. When I saw . . . her face swollen . . . the blood everywhere . . . the white of her skin . . .

ALBERTINE AT 40. Guilt . . .

ALBERTINE AT 60. I asked myself, is this where my life was leading? Is this the price I have to pay for a few years of peace? Is this the outcome . . . here, today? Did I bring her to this . . . my daughter . . . who I never knew how to manage? Or is it just to punish me? And for what? (*To* ALBERTINE AT 50.) For you?

ALBERTINE AT 50. No! It's not true!

ALBERTINE AT 60. Tough! If you're so naive to think that your life depends on you alone, too bad for you. You want to believe you have a choice, that you can choose to be free, that you can end your days making bacon, lettuce and sandwiches with mayo for a bunch of customers who will thank you till the end of time? Fine! Go right ahead! Let me know how it feels when the world comes crashing down around you, when you find yourself alone with nothing but guilt staring you in the face. Because that's the way we've always been had, and still we don't learn! You know what? I should have danced on my daughter's grave, yes danced, because at least, at least she chose her own destiny! (*She covers her mouth.*)

ALBERTINE AT 40. Is that why you started . . .

ALBERTINE AT 60. The pills? Let's say I was lucky to have an understanding doctor.

ALBERTINE AT 70. He told you not to overdo it . . .

ALBERTINE AT 60. I don't overdo it . . .

ALBERTINE AT 70. Not yet . . .

ALBERTINE AT 60. Sometimes I have no choice . . . It's that or insanity . . . I feel it coming . . . I can see Thérèse . . . Marcel too, who's drifted away for good . . . (*She stretches out her arms in a cross.*) The world . . . explodes! Rage comes back!

ALBERTINE AT 70. One day . . . or rather one night . . . the guilt will be too much . . . you'll take one too many . . .

ALBERTINE AT 60. Good! I'm glad! You never know, the door I open may lead to some place bearable. It can't be worse than here!

ALBERTINE AT 70 *looks around her.*

ALBERTINE AT 70. Mind you, you're right, it's not as bad. They're going to revive you, deintoxicate you, put you into a new 'home' as they say . . . They'll cure you of everything, except your memories . . .

MADELEINE. He's going to be late . . . That's what happens when he travels too far . . . I'm going in, it's cold . . .

ALBERTINE AT 30. I'll stay for a bit . . .

MADELEINE. You want a sweater?

ALBERTINE AT 30. Yes . . . Look, goosebumps . . .

MADELEINE. We'll talk tomorrow . . .

ALBERTINE AT 30. Yes, tomorrow . . .

MADELEINE (*looking out at the road*). If he gets home before you go to bed, tell him not to make any noise. If I'm asleep he won't wake me . . . and if I'm awake, I'll let him know one way or another . . .

ALBERTINE AT 70. Madeleine . . .

MADELEINE. Yes . . .

ALBERTINE AT 70. Don't worry about it . . . getting old's not worth it . . .

MADELEINE *goes out.*

Silence.

ALBERTINE AT 40 *prepares to go into the house.* ALBERTINE AT 50 *wipes her counter top. With difficulty,* ALBERTINE AT 60 *opens her container of pills.* ALBERTINE AT 70 *sighs.*

ALBERTINE AT 30. All alone in the middle of the world.

ALBERTINE AT 50. I'll do anything to keep that from happening! Anything!

ALBERTINE AT 60. Good luck . . .

ALBERTINE AT 40. If only Thérèse would come home . . . Please, don't let her do something crazy tonight . . .

ALBERTINE AT 70. Nothing will happen now . . . Mind you, that's just as well . . . an empty woman in front of an empty television in an empty room that doesn't smell good. (*Silence*.) Is this what you call a full life?

Silence.

ALBERTINE AT 50. Look . . .

ALBERTINE AT 40. What?

ALBERTINE AT 50. There she is . . . the moon.

The five ALBERTINES *look at the sky.*

ALBERTINE AT 60. I can't see it . . . Where did I put my glasses . . . (*She finds them and puts them on.*)

ALBERTINE AT 70. It's beautiful . . .

ALBERTINE AT 40. Yes, beautiful . . . even from here.

ALBERTINE AT 30. It's so big.

ALBERTINE AT 60. . . . and red . . .

Silence.

ALBERTINE AT 50. You could almost reach out and touch it . . .

ALBERTINE AT 60. She's alone, too.

The five ALBERTINES *slowly raise their arms toward the moon.*

ALBERTINE AT 70. Touch it . . . maybe it's the same one . . .

ALL FIVE ALBERTINES (*as if they had made physical contact*). Ahhhhh . . .

The moon, solitary and blood red, rises.

Blackout.

STAGE HISTORIES
AND CHRONOLOGY

Stage Histories

Les Belles Soeurs

Written in 1965.

Staged in 1968 at the Théâtre du Rideau Vert in Montreal, directed by André Brassard. The Rideau Vert, founded in 1948, was a mainstream theatre known for producing classics and with a rising commitment in the sixties to Quebec writing. It was an instant 'succès de scandale', shooting the young Tremblay into celebrity status. The critic Martial Dassylva declared Tremblay to be 'A talented dramatic writer possessed of extraordinary gifts of observation . . . However, considering the coarseness and vulgarity of this play, I can't help but think the Rideau Vert has done him a disservice by agreeing to produce it.'

English-language premiere at Toronto's St Lawrence Centre (seating capacity 830), the rough equivalent to London's National Theatre, in April 1973.

Staged in Paris at the Espace Pierre Cardin in late 1973, where it received rave reviews and was named best foreign play of the year.

Since then it has been performed throughout Canada and in the United States and shown on American television by CBC-TV in March 1978. It regularly appears on school curricula and is generally regarded as a classic of modern Quebec theatre.

British premiere, at the Tron theatre (seating capacity 230) as part of the Glasgow Mayfest 1989, in a new Scots translation entitled *The Guid Sisters*. It ran from 2–14 May and then 23–4 June. The Tron is one of Glasgow's leading alternative fringe theatres with a commitment to presenting contemporary and newly commissioned work and also to providing a home for small and middle-scale companies from the British Isles and abroad. *The Guid Sisters* played to good reviews and full houses: V. Gordon Smith, writing for the *Observer Scotland*, said, '(The Tron) should hire the biggest halls in the land and run it till the bus parties stop rolling, and make enough money to turn their inadequate home into the playhouse they deserve,' while the *Independent* called it 'theatre that is popular but not patronising'. Revived in May 1990 at the Clyde Theatre, Glasgow, (capacity 750) and then

went on to be the sole British entry at the du Maurier Ltd World
Stage Festival at the Harbourfront in Toronto, where it was again
very well received. A Yorkshire version by Noel Greig, *The Good
Sisters*, was premiered at the Crucible Theatre, Sheffield, on 23
May 1991.

Manon/Sandra

Written in 1977.
Staged at the Théâtre de Quat'Sous in Montreal (seating capacity
160), director André Brassard.
English-language premiere at the Mount Saint Vincent University
in Halifax in 1978 and performed at the Tarragon Theatre
(seating capacity 210) in Toronto in 1979, director Bill Glassco.
The Tarragon is similar to London's Royal Court in its policy of
producing new work and encouraging indigenous writing.
Although originally a fringe venue it is now regarded as a
mainstream theatre, again in much the same way that the Court is
now listed as a West End theatre.
British premiere at the Edinburgh Traverse in 1984. The Traverse
is a respected alternative theatre venue committed to presenting
'new theatre work that would not otherwise be presented for
commercial reasons'.
Revived at the Man in the Moon pub theatre (seating capacity 68),
a well-known London fringe theatre, in 1989 under the title
Manon/Sandra. It was directed by David Oliver Craik and staged by
the Nightingale Company and played to mixed reviews.

Albertine in Five Times

Written in 1984.
Staged at the National Arts Centre, Ottawa (seating capacity main
theatre 969, studio theatre 350), director André Brassard. This is a
mainstream theatre in the political capital of Canada with a
mandate to 'develop the performing arts in the National Capital
region, and to assist the Canada Council in the development of
the performing arts elsewhere in Canada'. Played to mixed
reviews.
English-language premiere at the Tarragon Theatre, Toronto,
directed by Bill Glassco. Went on to win a Chalmers Canadian
Plays Award for 1985; this is awarded to 'the most outstanding
Canadian plays produced professionally during the preceding
calendar year in the Metropolitan Toronto area.'
The Tarragon production of *Albertine* toured to Edinburgh where
it was given warm reviews; the *Scotsman* called it 'a moving version

of a delicate, beautiful play' and *The Times* referred to 'a
beautifully orchestrated production. The production transferred to
the Donmar Warehouse (seating capacity 248) in London where it
played for a week, again to good reviews.
It has also been produced in Caracas, Venezuela and Stockholm
as well as in the United States.

Chronology of Professionally Produced Plays

	French-language Premiere	English-language Premier	British Premiere
Le Train	1964		
Messe noire	1965		
Cinq	1966		
Les Belles-Soeurs	28. 8.68	3. 4.73	2.5.89
En Pièce Détachées	22. 4.69	1.73	
La Duchesse de Langeais	Spring 1969		
Demain matin, Montréal m'attend	4. 8.70		
Les Paons	11. 2.71		
A toi pour toujours ta Marie Lou	29. 4.71	4.10.72	
Hosanna	10. 5.73	5.74	14.5.91
Bonjour, là!, Bonjour	22. 8.74	3.75	
Surprise! Surprise	15. 4.75	30.10.75	
Les Héros de Mon Enfance	26. 6.76		
Sainte Carmen de la Main	20. 7.76	1.78	
Damnée Manon/Sacrée Sandra	24. 2.77	19. 4.79	11.8.84
L'Impromptu d'Outremont	11. 4.80	8. 5.80	
Les Grandes Vacances	10. 9.81		
Les Anciennes Odeurs	4.11.81		
Albertine, en cinq temps	12.10.84	9. 4.85	8.86
Le Vrai Monde?	2. 4.87	24. 5.88	5.89
La Maison Suspendue	1990		